Praise for Richard Lederer

Richard Lederer has done it again—another delightful, witty, and hugely absorbing celebration of the English language. Is there no stopping this man? – Bill Bryson, author of *The Mother Tongue*

Richard Lederer is to wordplay what John Philip Sousa is to marches. – Rod L. Evans, author of *Tyrannosaurus Lex*

Richard Lederer ought to be declared a national treasure. No one has more fun with the English language. – *Richmond Times Dispatch*

Richard Lederer is the true King of Language Comedy. –Sidney Sheldon, author of *After the Darkness*

Also by Richard Lederer

Adventures of a Verbivore
Amazing Words
American Trivia (with Caroline McCullagh)
American Trivia Quiz Book (with Caroline McCullagh)
Anguished English
Animal Cracker Uppers Jr. (with Jim Ertner)
The Ants Are My Friends (with Stan Kegel)
Basic Verbal Skills (with Philip Burnham)
The Big Book of Word Play Crosswords (with Gayle Dean)
The Bride of Anguished English
Building Bridge (with Bo Schambelan and Arnold Fisher)
Challenging Words for Smart People
The Circus of Words
Cleverly Comical Animal Jokes (with Jim Ertner)
Comma Sense (with John Shore)
Crazy English
The Cunning Linguist
Fractured English
Get Thee to a Punnery
The Giant Book of Animal Jokes (with Jim Ertner)
The Gift of Age
Hilarious Holiday Humor (with Stan Kegel)
The Joy of Names
Lederer on Language
Literary Trivia
A Man of My Words
The Miracle of Language
Monsters Unchained!

More Anguished English
The Play of Words
Presidential Trivia
Pun & Games
The Revenge of Anguished English
Rip Roaring Animal Jokes (with Jim Ertner)
Sleeping Dogs Don't Lay (with Richard Dowis)
Super Funny Animal Jokes (with Jim Ertner)
Theme and Paragraph (with Philip Burnham)
A Treasury for Cat Lovers
A Treasury for Dog Lovers
A Treasury of Christmas Humor
A Treasury of Halloween Humor
A Tribute to Teachers
Wild & Wacky Animal Jokes (with Jim Ertner)
The Word Circus
Word Wizard
The Write Way (with Richard Dowis)

The Complete Pleasure of Word & Phrase Origins

Illuminating Stories about the Histories and Mysteries of Everyday Language

RICHARD LEDERER
AUTHOR OF *ANGUISHED ENGLISH*

to Caroline McCullagh, Eileen Breedlove, Charlie Patton,
Dave Clary, and Chip Taulbee,
who help make my books and columns the best that they can be

Copyright © 2022, 2024 by Richard Lederer

All rights reserved. This book or any portion thereof may not be reproduced or used in any manner whatsoever without the express written permission of the publisher except for the use of brief quotations in articles and book reviews.

ISBN-13: 978-1-957807-77-5 hardcover edition
ISBN-13: 978-1-962984-74-4 paperback edition
ISBN-13: 978-1-957807-78-2 ebook edition

Waterside Productions
2055 Oxford Ave
Cardiff, CA 92007
www.waterside.com

TABLE OF CONTENTS

Introduction.................................... xi

Metaphors Be With You 1
Are You Playing With a Full Deck?.................. 3
Crunching the Numbers............................. 6
Haunted Words................................... 10
☺Similes Draw a Lot of Smiles.................... 14

Body Language................................ 17
Organ Recital................................... 19
The Eyes Have It................................ 23
Handy-Dandy English............................. 25
The Tooth, the Whole Tooth, and Nothing But the Tooth 29
Words From the Heart............................ 33
Body of Knowledge............................... 36
☺Crazy English................................. 38

That's Entertainment! 41
Face the Music.................................. 43
Show Biz in the Limelight....................... 45
A Circus of Words............................... 48
☺Ana Gram the Juggler.......................... 52
☺The Palindromedary............................ 55
My Kids, the Poker Players...................... 59
☺We All Speak Movie Lines...................... 62

Noah's Ark **65**
Beastly Word Origins 67
The Bird Is the Word 75
☺Lions and Tigers and Bears 80
The Cat's Got Our Tongue 84
The Dog's Got Our Tongue 88
What's in a Name? 92
☺Animal Advice 94

Land, Sea, Air, and Beyond **97**
Down-to-Earth Metaphors 99
An Anthology of Flowery Words 102
Our Seaworthy Language 105
CANOE 110
Under the Weather 112
Plane Talk 115
Racing with the Moon, Dancing with the Stars 118
☺When Metaphors Collide 122

Food For Thought **125**
We Say a Mouthful 127
We Eat Our Words 130
☺Unappetizing Menus 132
☺What's In a Name? 135

Taking Care of Business **137**
English Means Business 139
Fighting Words 144
What's My Line? 149
Coining Phrases 153
☺You're Fired! 156
☺The Hello Name Game 158
☺Nothing Works for Me 161

Sports Illustrated	165
Our Sporty English Language	167
Ball's In Your Court	170
Par For the Course	173
Take Me Out to the Ballgame	176
☺A Guide to Sportspeak	179
Hats In the Ring	181
A Primer of Political Words	183
OK!	188
Teddy's Bear	190
☺Political Tickles	192
☺American History According to Student Bloopers	194
The Annals of Science	197
Brave New Words	199
Immortal Mortals	202
☺Science Fantasies	207
Classical Words	211
Latina Non Mortua Est	213
Dig Down to the Roots	218
A God is Hiding in Your Sentence	221
☺Mythic Riddles	225
It's About Time	228
Sacred Words	233
That Old-Time Religion	235
The True Meanings of Christmas	237
Gee Whiz!	241
☺Name That Tune!	243
☺Bible Riddles	246

Location, Location **249**
Putting Words In Their Places 251
Our Native American Heritage 256
☺Puns That Babylon. 259

Acknowledgments 263
Author Biography 265

Introduction

To the man or woman who knows its origin, each word presents a picture, no matter how ordinary it may appear. Exploring the history and mystery of words and phrases gives me the same pleasure I used to experience when my grandfather opened the family album, pointed to a cluster of sepia photographs, and told me stories about the people gazing out from the pages. Most were born long before we were, and all bequeath us their rich legacies. Illuminating the faded picture of a time-hallowed word or phrase throws light on our forebears and our customs, our working and our playing, and our fighting and our loving.

Has it ever struck you how human words are?

Like people, words are born, grow up, get married, have children, and even die. They may be very old, like *man* and *wife* and *home*. They may be very young, like *binge watching, selfie stick, emoji, hangry, clickbait, cryptocurrency,* and *EGOT*, the rare feat of winning an Emmy, Grammy, Oscar, and Tony. Or they may repose in the tomb of history, as *leechcraft*, the Anglo-Saxon word for the practice of medicine, and *murfles*, a long-defunct word for freckles or pimples.

Our lives are filled with people and words, and in both cases, we are bound to be impressed by their vast numbers and infinite variety. Some words, like *OK*, are famous all over the world. Others, like *foozle* (a bungling golf stroke) and *groak* (to stare at other people's food, hoping that they will offer you some), are scarcely known, even at home.

There are some words that we have probably never met, such as *samara* (the pinwheels that grow on maple trees) and *ferrule* (the metal band that holds an eraser to a pencil or the metal tip of an umbrella)

There are others that are with us every day of our lives, such as *the, be, to, of,* and *and,* the five most frequently used English words.

As with people, words have all sorts of shapes, sizes, backgrounds, and personalities. They may be very large, like *pneumonoultramicroscopicsilicovolcanoconiosis,* a forty-five-letter hippopotomonstrosesquipedalian word for black lung disease. They may be very small, like *a* and *I.*

Some words are multinational in their heritage, as *remacadamize,* which is Latin, Celtic, Hebrew, and Greek in parentage. Some come of Old English stock, as *sun* and *moon* and *grass* and *goodness.* Some have a distinctly continental flavor, like *lingerie, kindergarten,* and *spaghetti.* Others are unmistakably American, like *stunt* and *baseball.*

Words like *remunerative, encomium,* and *perspicacious* are so dignified that they can intimidate us, while others, like *booze, burp,* and *blubber,* are markedly inelegant in character. Some words, like *covidiot* and *palimony,* are winkingly playful. Other words strike us as beautiful—*luminous* and *gossamer.* Some words sound rather ugly—*guzzle* and *scrod;* some sound quiet—*dawn* and dusk—and others as noisy—*thunder* and *crash.*

Words, like people, go up and down in the world. Some are born into low station and come up in the life. With the passing of time, they may acquire *prestige* (which used to mean "trickery") and *glamour* (which began life as a synonym for *grammar*). Others slide downhill in reputation, such as *homely* (which originally meant "homelike; good around the home"), *villain* ("a member of the lower class"), and *idiot* ("a private citizen").

In the year 1666, a great fire swept through London and destroyed more than half the city, including three-quarters of St. Paul's Cathedral. Sir Christopher Wren, the original designer of

Introduction

the cathedral and perhaps the finest architect of all time, was commissioned to rebuild the great edifice. He began in 1675 and finished in 1710—a remarkably short time for such a task. When the grand project was completed, Queen Anne, the reigning monarch, visited the cathedral and told Wren that his work was "awful, artificial, and amusing." Sir Christopher, so the story goes, was delighted with the royal compliment, because in those days *awful* meant "full of awe, awe-inspiring," *artificial* meant "artistic," and *amusing*, from the Muses, meant "amazing."

You've just started a reading a book about etymology. The etymology of the word *etymology* is the Greek root *etymon*, "true, original," and the Greek ending *–logia*, "science or study." Etymology, then, is the science or study of true and original word meanings. An etymologist is one who knows the difference between etymology, the study of word histories, and entomology, the study of insects.

About the birth and lives of words I am enthusiastic, enchanted, ecstatic, exhilarated, exuberant, ebullient, and effervescent. Ah, those wonderful words that begin with *E*: In their early lives, *enthusiastic* meant "possessed by a god," *enchanted* "singing a magic song," *ecstatic* "in a trance," *exhilarated* "made thoroughly cheerful," and *exuberant*, *ebullient*, and *effervescent* "overflowing, boiling over, spouting out."

Carnivores eat meat; piscivores love fish; herbivores consume plants and vegetables; verbivores devour words. I am such a creature. My whole life I have feasted on words—ogled their appetizing shapes, colors, and textures; swished them around in my mouth; lingered over their many tastes; let their juices run down my chin. Now that you have progressed this far in this Introduction, you are clearly a fellow verbivore.

Words are who we are. Words are what we do. Words inspire our hearts, spark our minds, and beget our laughter. Words move the world. Words are as great a joy as food and drink. May *A Pleasury of Word & Phrase Origins* fill you with such palate-pleasing nourishment and ear-rinsing joy.

The source of that tingly sensation you feel when your arm strikes a foreign object is the knob on the end of the bone running from the shoulder to the elbow. The medical name for that bone is the *humerus,* and back in 1840, some clever wag seized upon the homophonic similarity between *humerus* and *humorous* and dubbed the humerus the *funny bone,* a learned pun that has become part of our language. Since then, we've found out that if you boil your funny bone, it becomes a humerus laughing stock.

To thrive in life, you need three bones: a wish bone, a back bone, and a funny bone. In each thematic cluster of this Pleasury, you'll see a smiley face—😊—or two. These emojis tell you that what follows will be a humorous take-off on the core subject of the cluster. I have installed these acts of comic relief to lighten up each theme and your life. Most books about etymology are solemn affairs. I, your fly-by-the roof of the mouth, user-friendly Wizard of Idiom, Abbot of Absurdity, and Attila the Pun, believe that learning should be dressed up to have fun. I fully subscribe to this bygone but timely children's rhyme:

> What's learned with pleasure
> Is learned full measure.

Richard Lederer
San Diego, California
richardhlederer@gmail.com
verbivore.com

METAPHORS BE WITH YOU

I'm behind the eight ball, so I guess I'll have to go back to ground zero —or should that be square one?

ARE YOU PLAYING WITH A FULL DECK?

Language is like the air we breathe. It's invisible. It's all around us. We can't get along without it. Yet we take it for granted. But when we step back and listen to the words that escape from the holes in our faces and luminesce up on our computer screens, we are in for a lifetime of joy.

Before you dive into this chapter, take a few minutes to write down all the adjectives you can think of to describe someone who is highly intelligent.

Chances are that among your answers are words like

> *bright* *acute*
> *brilliant* *clever*
> *dazzling* *incisive*
> *lucid* *keen*
> *scintillating* *sharp*

If you examine these two lists of adjectives, you'll notice that each clusters around a single basic concept. All the words on the left compare intelligence to light, including *scintillating*, which descends from the Latin *scintilla*, "a spark," and all the words on the right compare intelligence to the edge of a knife, including *clever*, which can be traced directly back to the Old English *cleave* and *cleaver*.

Such comparisons are called metaphors, and the English language never metaphor it didn't like. A metaphor (the word originally meant "carry beyond" in Greek) is a figure of speech that merges two objects or ideas that are, for the most part, different from each other but turn out to be alike in some significant way. In other words, metaphors tell it like it isn't to show us what it really is. We usually think of metaphors as figurative devices that only poets create, but, in fact, all of us make metaphors during almost every moment of our waking lives. As T. E. Hulme observed, "Prose is a museum, where all the old weapons of poetry are kept." Ralph Waldo Emerson put it this way: "The etymologist finds the deadest word to have been once a brilliant picture. Language is fossil poetry."

Now that you've analyzed metaphors that spotlight substantial brainpower, think of the tag phrases we use to identify loopy, wifty, wiggy people who are short on intelligence, judgment, or sanity. The best-known of these metaphors is "He/she isn't playing with a full deck." In fact, these metaphors have come to be called "full deckisms." Here follow a half dozen clusters of these jocular figurative comparisons:

Light metaphors. The light's on, but nobody's home. He's a dim bulb in the marquee of life. She's not the brightest bulb on the Christmas tree. He's so dense that light bends around him. She's so dumb her psychiatrist carries a flashlight.

Food metaphors. He's one pickle short of a full jar, two sandwiches short of a picnic, two cans short of a six-pack, and a french fry short of a Happy Meal. She's nutty as a fruitcake. His kernel never popped. The butter slipped off her noodle. He's not cooking on all burners. There aren't any beans in her pod. He puts mustard on his Froot Loops. Somebody blew out her pilot light. He takes an hour to cook Minute Rice. If brains were chocolate, he wouldn't have enough to fill an M&M. She's all foam and no beer. He's slow as molasses in January. She didn't drink from the fountain of knowledge; she just gargled.

Nautical metaphors. He doesn't have both oars in the water. Her line's in the water, but the bait's missing. He hasn't packed a full sea bag. The wind is blowing, but nothing is moving. She has a Titanic intellect in a world of icebergs. He's a submarine with a screen door. Her mooring lines don't reach the dock. There's no hand on his rudder.

Automotive metaphors. His brain is stuck in first gear. Her tank is a quart low. His motor isn't firing on all cylinders. Her battery is dead. He's running on empty. She's driving in reverse. He's got one wheel in the sand. Her wipers don't touch the glass. He has a leak in the think tank. Her tires are low. His clutch is slipping. If brains were gasoline, he wouldn't have enough to drive a dinky car around the inside of a Cheerio. She missed her last four scheduled tune-ups.

Building metaphors. His elevator doesn't go all the way to the top. She's one brick short of a full load. He has a few screws loose. Her brain is an unfurnished room for rent. The top rung of his ladder is missing. She's a bubble off plumb. His gate's off its hinges. Her fence doesn't have all its pickets. He has termites in his attic. Her driveway doesn't reach the road. He's long on drywall and short on studs.

Computer metaphors. She's one chip short of a megabyte. He has a 10K brain attached to a 9600-baud mouth. She has a terabyte drive, but data on punch cards. His is a vacuum-tube brain in a microchip world. She is an experiment in artificial stupidity. His files are compressed one hundred percent. Her data bus stops for red lights.

I'm an octogenarian, but I'm still playing with a full deck. I do notice, however, that the cards shuffle more slowly.

Crunching the Numbers

To give you some sense of what this book does, let's crunch some numbers. It is not only the mathematician who is fascinated by numbers. Whether we know it or not, we all speak numbers, from zero through ten, and well beyond. It's as easy as one-two-three.

From time to time, I hear people say, "That didn't work. I guess we'll have to go back to ground zero." *Ground zero* is a fairly new compound in English. It refers to the point on the Earth's surface closest to a detonation. The term was first used in 1946 to refer to Hiroshima and Nagasaki, Japan, the sites of nuclear detonations in World War II. It broadened its meaning to mean any detonation site, and now any site that is a center of activity. When capitalized, as in "Ground Zero," it refers to the former site of the Twin Towers in New York City.

People often confuse *ground zero* with the more logical phrase *I guess we'll have to go back to square one*. Here the metaphor is probably rooted in the playground game four-square, which first appeared in the early 1950s. A player starts in square one and tries to move through squares two and three to square four by hitting an unreturnable ball into one of the other squares. The losing player goes back to square one.

Hidden forms of the number two occur in the words *between, betwixt, combine, zwieback,* and *twilight,* in which *tween, twixt, bi, zwie,* and *twi* all mean "two." The root sense of *zwieback* is "twice baked," of *biscuit* "twice cooked," and of *combine* "to join two things." Twilight is literally the time of two lights, the fading sunset and the emerging light of the stars. In the old days, before the creation of artificial light brighter than a candle, the light of the stars was very bright after the sun went down.

Thanks to the game of Trivial Pursuit and a stack of general-knowledge quiz books, Americans have been learning all sorts of exotic and arcane facts, from *aardvark,* a large, burrowing, nocturnal mammal and the first noun in most dictionaries, to *zyzzyva,* a genus of tropical South American snouted weevil discovered in Brazil. With the first five of its seven letters being z or y, *zyzzyva* has the last word in many dictionaries. No longer than an ant, this insect could be labeled "the lesser of two weevils."

The word *trivia,* meaning "things of little or no importance," is borrowed from the neuter plural of the Latin *trivium,* "a place where three roads meet" and exchange idle chitchat. *Trivium* took on a more metaphorical significance in the Middle Ages, when it referred to the three roads to knowledge—Grammar, Rhetoric, and Logic.

Writer James Joyce is said to have said, "My puns are not trivial. They are quadrivial."

In the eighteenth century, the three estates of a realm were the nobility, the clergy, and the common people. In modern times, because of its watchdog responsibilities, which are crucial to a functioning democracy, the press is considered the Fourth Estate.

Now let's take five for the number five. It's easy to see that the *quint* in *quintet* and *quintuplets* means "five." Less apparent is the *quint* in *quintessence.* The ancient Greeks held that everything in the world was composed of four elements—earth, air, fire, and water. To these the philosopher Aristotle added a new element, which the Roman philosopher and statesman Cicero dubbed *quinta essentia,* "fifth essence," higher and purer than the four earthly elements. William Shakespeare's Prince Hamlet uses the word that way when he laments, "What a piece of work is man, how noble in reason, how infinite in faculties...And yet, to me, what is this quintessence of dust?"

Siesta, from the Latin compound *sexta hora,* literally means "the sixth hour after sunrise, i.e. 'noon'," but the *siesta* now refers to a rest period that can occur at any time of day.

In Islam, the belief is that there exist seven levels of heaven, the highest being the *seventh heaven,* where God and the most exalted angels dwell. As a result, *seventh heaven* now means "a state of intense happiness," as in "I'm in seventh heaven learning so many new word and phrase origins."

The best-known expression involving the number eight is *behind the eight ball.* In Kelly pool, up to fifteen players may participate. They draw numbers out of a bottle to determine the order of play. Any player past eight has little chance of winning. *Behind the eight ball* has been generalized to mean "any difficult, troublesome situation."

The fact that no printed citation exists for *the whole nine yards* prior to 1967 renders dubious the nautical theory that the expression refers to the nine sails on a three-masted square rigger. Nor could *the whole nine yards,* which means "the whole shootin' match," "whole hog," "the whole ball of wax," and "the whole enchilada," issue from football, in which a team must gain ten, not nine, yards to reach a first down. Equally unproven or provably wrong are dozens of other etymological explanations, including the material to make a dress, bridal veil, or Scottish kilt; the length of a machine-gun belt in World War II fighter planes; the height of a prison wall; and the volume of mined ore.

My research has revealed that *the whole nine yards* refers to the revolving barrels on the backs of concrete mixing trucks. Those barrels held a volume of nine cubic yards in the early 1960s, a fact that I thought explained why I had never heard the phrase when I was growing up in the 1950s.

As you can see, my explanations are never in the abstract—and always in the concrete.

Hardee har har! But *au contraire,* take a chill pill and hold your horses. Turns out that *the whole nine yards* popped up in an Indiana newspaper article way back in 1855! That's why Yale University librarian Fred R. Shapiro describes the expression, with its duffle bag stuffed with conjectures about its origins, as "the most prominent etymological riddle of our time."

CRUNCHING THE NUMBERS

Dec is the Latin root for "ten," as in *decade, decimal,* and *decimate. To decimate* once described the nasty habit of the Roman commanders of slaying one out of every ten soldiers, selected by lot, in a mutinous legion. Nowadays *decimate* means "to destroy a large number of living things," with no connection to the number ten, as in "the gypsy moth caterpillars decimated the trees in our yard."

Clearly, the days of our English language have long been numbered, twenty-four/seven.

HAUNTED WORDS

The proud house of etymology is populated by all manner of ghoulies and ghosties and long-leggety beasties spawned by spook etymologists. (*Spook* reaches back to the Dutch *spooc,* "ghost, specter.") These sham scholars would rather invent a word origin after the fact than trace it to its true source. Spooks prefer drama and romance to accuracy and truth.

Caveat lexophile: Word lover beware.

Sirloin is not so called because James I or Henry VIII (according to Thomas Fuller in 1655) or Charles II (according to *Cook's Oracle* in 1822) knighted his favorite dish, declaring, "Arise, Sir Loin." In truth, *sirloin,* the upper or choicer part of a loin of beef, was borrowed from Middle French *surloigne* (*sur,* "above" + *loigne,* "loin") centuries before any of the monarchs who are credited with honoring the cut of meat. But legends die hard, especially when they are lit by such bright stories, and this particular flight of etymological fancy has survived for more than three centuries as a hoax of word play foisted on unsuspecting language lovers.

Another meaty phrase origin that I feel compelled to beef and stew about is *to give someone the cold shoulder.* In days of yore, guests were treated hospitably to meals that included generous cuts of warm mutton and beef. But when they had overstayed their welcome, the hosts would serve up cold shoulders of leftover and often inferior cuts, signaling that the time had come to leave.

Such a vivid and palatable explanation of the phrase, but it's not true. Walter Scott, who, some say, invented the expression, wrote in *St. Ronan's Well,* "Ye may mind that the Countess's dislike did na gang farther at first than just shewing o' the cauld ['cold'] shouther ['shoulder']. Note that Scott expresses neither eating nor food in this passage. *To give someone the cold shoulder* simply means and comes from the idea of cold indifference or rejection expressed by turning away from the recipient of such a spurning, akin *to giving a thumbs down.*

Spook etymologies are haunting your computer, in the form of a ubiquitous item titled "Life in the 1500s," which has been dragging its chains around the internet for years. The color and romance of the word and phrase explanations in the message are as beguiling as can be. One of them is this electronic explanation of a common meteorological phrase: "Houses had thatched roofs. Thick straw, piled high, with no wood underneath. It was the only place for animals to get warm, so all the pets—dogs, cats, mice, rats, and bugs—lived in the roof. When it rained, it became slippery, and sometimes the animals would slip and fall off the roof. Hence the saying *It's raining cats and dogs.*"

Folderol! Piffle! Poppycock! The truth appears to be more mundane. Cats and dogs make a lot of noise when they fight (hence, "fighting like cats and dogs"), so they have become a metaphor for a noisy rain or thunderstorm.

Now the plot deepens, and our subject turns grave. Hear ye now the most ghoulish and foolish of the spook etymologies that clank throughout this disquisition: "England is old and small, and they started running out of places to bury people. So they would dig up coffins and would take their bones to a house and reuse the grave. In reopening these coffins, one out of twenty-five coffins were found to have scratch marks on the inside, and they realized they had been burying people alive. So they thought they would tie a string on the wrist of the corpse, lead it through the coffin and up through the ground, and tie it to a bell. Someone would have to sit out in the graveyard all night to listen for the bell. Hence the expression *graveyard shift.* They would know that someone was *saved by the bell* or he was *a dead ringer.*"

Hogwash! Hooey! Humbug! Despite high marks for ingenuity, these etymological explanations are merely exercises in free association without regard for attribution. In factories that work around the clock, employees report for work at 8 a.m. for the "regular" or "day" shift; at 4 p.m. for the "swing" or "night" shift; and at midnight for the "graveyard" shift, lasting until 8 a.m. According to Harold Wentworth and Stuart Berg Flexner's *Dictionary of American Slang*, the name *graveyard shift* refers to "the ghostlike hour of employment"—and nothing more.

Dead ringers actually originated at the racetrack. To take advantage of the long odds against an inferior horse's winning a race, unscrupulous gamblers would substitute a horse of superior ability and similar appearance. Nowadays, *dead ringer* means any close look-alike.

Why *ringer*? Probably because *ringer* was once a slang term for a counterfeiter who represented brass rings as gold ones at county fairs. And *dead* here means "absolute, exact," as in "dead heat" and "you're dead right."

Should I even dignify the windy suspiration about *saved by the bell* with a logical explanation? Oh well, here 'tis, and it's just what you thought in the first place. *Saved by the bell* is nothing more than the obvious—a reference to the bell signaling the end of a round of boxing. No matter what condition a fighter is in during a boxing match, even if they are being counted out, they are saved by the bell and gain a reprieve once that bell rings.

An acronym (Greek *akros*, "tip," as in *acrobat* and *acrophobia* + *onyma*, "name") is a word formed from the first letters (tips) of other words. Always beware and be wary of acronymic etymologies. *Cop* does not stand for "*c*onstable *o*n *p*atrol," nor *tip*, as a gratuity, for "*t*o *i*nsure *p*romptness," nor *news* for "*n*orth-*e*ast-*w*est-*s*outh," nor *golf* for "*g*entlemen *o*nly, *l*adies *f*orbidden," nor you-know-what for "*f*or *u*nlawful *c*arnal *k*nowledge."

I fervently hope that we all gain a reprieve from these bamboozling spook etymologies that rattle and clank around the internet and haunt the halls of our language. That, of course, is the same internet that informs us that National Public Radio is about to go out of business; that Congress is about to institute an e-mail tax; that a virus is about to crash your computer; that your toilet is about to explode; that antiperspirants, Canola Oil, and NutraSweet cause just about every malady known to humankind; that a Nigerian businessman will make you rich if you will just make a modest deposit in his account; that four hundred and fifty years ago Nostradamus predicted the outcome of our presidential elections, 9/11, and other history-changing events; and that next July we collide with Mars. If you believe everything you glean from cyberspace, especially about language, please get in touch with me. I have a bridge, a lovely parcel of swampland, and a subprime mortgage I want to sell you.

😊Similes Draw a Lot of Smiles

A simile is a figure of speech that compares two essentially different objects or ideas, expressly indicated by words such as *like* or *as*, as in:

- O my love is like a red, red rose that's newly sprung in June. / O my love is like the melody that's sweetly played in tune. – *Robert Burns*
- Life is like a box of chocolates. You never know what you're gonna get. – *Winston Groom*
- Life is like a roll of toilet paper. The closer it gets to the end, the faster it spins. – *Anonymous*
- What happens to a dream deferred? / Does it dry up / like a raisin in the sun? / Or fester like a sore / —And then run? – *Langston Hughes*
- A woman needs a man like a fish needs a bicycle –*Irina Dunn*
- Life is like a dog sled race. If you're not the lead dog, the scenery never changes. – *Anonymous*
- Marriage is like a deck of cards. You start off with two hearts and a diamond, and pretty soon you want to grab a club and use a spade. – *Richard Lederer*

Finally, we may well wonder why people say *naked as a jaybird* when jaybirds are covered with feathers. Here's the first printed citation of *naked as a jaybird* as it appeared in 1893: "He will have the humbug qualifications of a cow-boy stripped from his poor worthless carcass so quickly that he would feel like a jay bird with his tail feathers gone." Turns out, therefore, that a jaybird is naked when its nether plumage is missing.

Because animals can't hire public relations agents, they often get bum raps in many of our common similes:

- *Blind as a bat.* Actually, bats aren't blind. Some, flying at night, use echolocation, a form of natural sonar, to find their prey, but they can also see. Others, such as fruit bats, fly in the daytime, using their sharp eyes to get around.
- *Sweat like a pig.* Unlike humans, who perspire through approximately 2.6 million sweat glands, pigs possess few sweat glands, so they can't sweat effectively. Instead, they cool off by rolling in mud. It's possible that this swinish simile derives from cooling pig iron bars, which form droplets in the process.
- *Slimy as a snake.* Although a snake's scales are shiny and may appear slimy, the reptile's body is dry to the touch. A few amphibians, such as some frogs and salamanders, are slimy, but snakes aren't.

You've probably heard the expression *slow as molasses (in January)*. But molasses isn't slow. In the Boston Molasses Disaster of 1919, a massive vat of molasses collapsed on a warm day, producing a twenty-five-foot-high wave that swept through neighborhoods at thirty-five miles per hour. Twenty-five people perished on that bittersweet day.

Speaking of similes, Judge Martin J. Sheehan, of Kenton County, Kentucky, Circuit Court, waxed figuratively about the settlement of a case that had been scheduled to go to trial:

> And such news of an amicable settlement having made this court happier than a tick on a fat dog because it is otherwise busier than a one-legged cat in a sand box and, quite frankly, would have rather jumped naked off of a twelve-foot

step ladder and into a five-gallon bucket of porcupines than have presided over a two-week trial of the herein dispute, a trial which, no doubt, would have made the jury more confused than a hungry baby in a topless bar and made the parties and their attorneys madder than mosquitoes in a mannequin factory.

It is therefore ordered and adjudicated that the jury trial scheduled herein for July 13, 2011, is hereby canceled.

I now bid you adieu with a series of punderful similes: It's time for me to make like a tree and leave, make like a bee and buzz off, make like an airplane and take off, make like a boatman and shove off, make like an amoeba and split, make like a nose and run, make like a hurricane and blow this popsicle stand, make like a dog and flea, make like a nut and bolt, make like the Red Sea and part, make like a tire and hit the road, make like a hat and go on a head, make like a bakery truck and haul buns, make like deodorant and roll on, make like a quarterback and take a hike, make like peanut butter and jam, make like a sock in the dryer and get lost, make like a shepherd and get the flock out of here, make like the Invisible Man and disappear, make like Michael Jackson and "Beat It!," make like Ella Fitzgerald and scat, make like Johann Strauss and waltz out of here, and make like an Amazon customer and say, "Good buy!"

Body Language

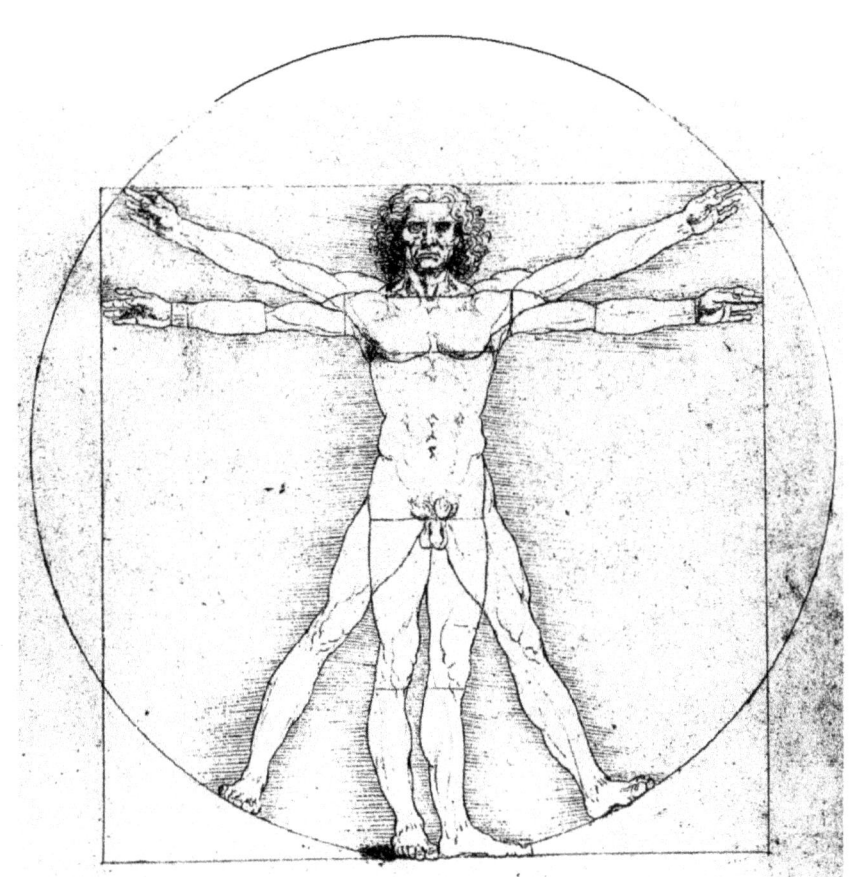

ORGAN RECITAL

An old American folk rhyme chuckles:

> Where can a man find a cap for his knee,
> Or a key for a lock of his hair?
> Can his two eyes be called an academy
> Because there are pupils in there?
>
> In the crown of his head, what gems are set?
> Who travels the bridge of his nose?
> Can he use, when shingling the roof of his mouth,
> The nails on the ends of his toes?
>
> What does he raise from a slip of his tongue.
> And who beats the drums of his ears?
> And who can tell the cut and the style
> Of the coat his stomach wears?
>
> Can the crooks of his elbows be sent to jail.
> And if so, just what did they do?
> And how does he sharpen his shoulder blades?
> I'll be darned if I know. Do you?

Metaphors are a way of explaining the abstract in terms of the concrete. Small wonder that we take our most common metaphors from things that surround us in our daily lives and find a rich vein of descriptive phrases about the most familiar presence—our own bodies. We metaphorically talk and write about *the long arm of the law, I've got your back, the backbone of democracy, fire in the belly, body of knowledge, a bare-bones report, knit your brow, bosom buddy, a no-brainer, take it on the chin, a clean breast of things, turn the other cheek, get it off your chest, sticks in your craw, crotch of a tree, dog-eared pages, elbow grease, eye of a needle, to raise eyebrows, save face, put my finger on, flesh out, two-fisted, foot the bill, a gut-wrenching experience, hair's breadth, hamstrung, hands of a clock, head of lettuce, heart of the matter, Achilles heel, intestinal fortitude, joined at the hip, jaw-dropping, kidney bean, knee-jerk reaction, knuckle under, the lap of luxury* (a lap is a body part, but only when you sit down), *leg of a journey, to risk life and limb, stiff upper lip, mouth of a river, a nail-biter, hard-nosed, breakneck speed, strike a nerve, rib-tickling, side-splitting humor, shoulder of a road, spine of a book, rule of thumb, toe the line, tongue of a shoe, sweet tooth*—you get the idea.

And think about the body parts we employ to insult others, as in "there are more *horse's asses* in the world than there are horses." Other pejorative corporeal putdowns include *armpit of the nation, backbiting, yellow-bellied, bonehead, busybody, lame brain, butt ugly, cheeky, chin music, tin ear, four eyes, crow's feet, give the finger to, gutless, ham-fisted, heavy-handed, headstrong, knucklehead, lily-livered, pay lip service, hard-hearted, knock kneed, blabbermouth, muscle head, redneck, you have a lot of nerve, sticks her nose in other people's business, numb nuts, ticket scalper, gives the cold shoulder, skeletons in the closet, numbskull, spineless, I can't stomach political shenanigans, thin skinned, thunder thighs, cutthroat, snaggletooth, pantywaist,* and *limp-wristed.*

England doesn't have a kidney bank, but it does have a Liverpool

The ancients, in their finite wisdom, believed that the womb—*hystera* in Greek, "womb"—was an unfixed organ that floated around inside a woman's body, tickling her and making her emotionally unstable, or *hysterical.* In that sense, *hysteria* is a subtle dig at women, stereotyping them as flighty and emotionally volatile. It was

Sigmund Freud who first popularized the notion that men could be hysterical, too.

Moving from a female-directed word to one that is male-oriented, you may be surprised to learn that the Old and New Testaments of the Bible include testicles. The Latin for "witness" being *testis*, the Testaments testify ("bear witness") to God's truth. *Testis* is the same root that yields *protest*, "to bear witness for"; *detest*, "to bear witness against"; and *contest*, "to bear witness competitively."

In Latin, *testiculi* means "little witnesses" because that part of a man's body testified to the bearer's virility. Men once placed their hands on their precious gonads to swear the truth, the whole truth, and nothing but the truth. Witness Genesis 24: 2, 3, and 9: "And Abraham said unto his eldest servant of his house, that ruled over all he had, Put, I pray thee, thy hand under my thigh, And I will make thee swear by the Lord, the God of heaven, and the God of earth, that thou shalt not take a wife unto my son of the daughters of the Canaanites, among whom I dwell...And the servant put his hand under the thigh [also translated from the Hebrew *yarek* as 'soft bits'] of Abraham his master and sware to him concerning the matter."

Why is it, I wonder, that a man gets a *her*nia and a woman a *hy*sterectomy?

The word *temple* derives from the Latin *tempus,* which means "time." Why? Because the hair that grows over the temples on each side of your head is often the first area to turn gray from age, a visible sign the passage of time.

Today's announcers and athletes sometimes use the word *podium* as a verb, as in "Simone Bales will certainly podium in the floor exercise." This reminds us that a *podium,* from the Greek *podion,* "foot," which is rooted in *podiatrist* and evolves into *pedestrian* through Latin, is a block of wood upon which stand athletes, orchestra, conductors, and speakers. But nowadays, we hear the likes of "Senator Mudslinger is walking up onto the podium. Now he steps onto the podium and lays his notes on the podium."

What goes here? How could Senator Mudslinger stoop so low? Can a podium be a stage, a small base, and a slant-topped desk behind which speakers stand and on which they place their notes?

Apparently, a podium can be all these things, but for folks like me, a *lectern* (from the Latin *legers,* "to read") is the slant-topped desk, a *podium* a small base behind a lectern, and the whole stage a *platform, dais,* or *rostrum.*

And always remember to keep your eyes on the prize, your nose to the grindstone, your shoulder to the wheel, your hand on the tiller, your face to the wind, your chin up, your ear to the ground, and your foot on the pedal. Then go see your chiropractor.

The Eyes Have It

We see the importance of the eyes in the many expressions and proverbs that speak of them: "The mind's eye." "In the blink of an eye." "Eyes on the prize." "Here's mud in your eye." "An eye for an eye and a tooth for a tooth." "Love is blind." "Beauty is in the eye of the beholder." "Out of sight, out of mind." "The night has a thousand eyes." "The eyes are bigger than the stomach." "Don't give me the stink eye." "Turn a blind eye to." "In the land of the blind, the one-eyed man is king." "I won't pull the wool over your eyes." "Even a blind squirrel finds a nut." Many an eye-catching, bright-eyed and bushy-tailed word and phrase is a sight for sore eyes and hits the bull's-eye.

> What did one eye say to the other eye? *Between you and me, something smells.*
> Have you heard about the cross-eyed teacher? *She couldn't control her pupils.*

That last prey on words plays on the two meanings of the word *pupil*. The first, "a student," is borrowed from the Latin *pupillus*, "orphan, ward, minor." A second meaning boasts a more enchanting etymology: In ancient Rome, the *papilla*, "little doll," was a diminutive of *pupa*, "girl." When the Romans looked deep into each other's eyes, they used the same word for the tiny doll-like images of themselves reflected there. They called the part of the eye that the image could be seen in the *pupil*.

Daylights is timeworn slang for the human eyes, dating back to at least the early eighteenth century. This makes a certain amount of sense since the eyes are the "source" of all the light we see. The practice of equating the eyes with lights or windows is even older; one Latin word for *eye* was *lumen,* meaning "light." To beat or scare the daylights out of someone first meant to pummel or frighten them so badly that their eyes, at least figuratively, popped out.

A Yiddish proverb tells us that "the eyes are the windows of the soul." In Middle English, *window* was born as Old Norse *vindagauga,* "the wind's eye," a feature of a home that let out the eye-stinging smoke and odor of bodies and damp fur.

An *autopsy*—Greek *auto,* "self" + *opsy,* "eye"—is an examination of a dead person in which the coroner sees with his or her own eyes.

The adjective *supercilious,* literally "with raised eyebrows," issues from the Latin *super,* "above," and *cilium,* "eyelid." Supercilious people are highbrows who display haughtiness and condescension by raising an eyebrow and looking down their nose at you.

If you "make eyes" at someone, you are *ogling* them, from *oghe,* a Middle Dutch word for "eye."

Please remember that in life it's better to be optimistic than to be misty-optic.

Handy-Dandy English

Mano a mano, you have to hand it to our handy English language. You may think that *mano a mano* means "man to man," but it doesn't. It means "hand-to-hand," as in "hand-to-hand combat."

In *The Social Conquest of the Earth,* eminent biologist E. O. Wilson explains the spectacular success of human beings in mastering our planet. The formula for achieving such total global dominance requires that you be a large terrestrial animal and that you forget paws, claws, or hooves. Instead, acquire "grasping hands tipped with soft spatulate fingers."

Our hands, with their flexible digits and opposable thumbs, help us to size up and manipulate the world around us. "The integrative powers of the brain for the sensations that come from handling objects," says Wilson, "spill out into all other domains of intelligence." No wonder, then, that hands leave their fingerprints all over the words and phrases we speak and hear and write and read every day.

I try to be even-handed in my approach to writing. I try not to be a high-handed, underhanded, heavy-handed knucklehead or one who glad-hands. I don't want you to handcuff me or force my hand or reject my writing out of hand. Please give me a free hand to show my hand by presenting for your consideration a handy-dandy, two-fisted topic about which I possess firsthand knowledge and know like the back of my hand.

President Harry Truman loved to tell a joke about the dismal science of economics: "All my economists say, 'on the one hand... on the other hand.' Just give me a one-handed economist!" The quip depends on one's sense of the hand as a pervasive metaphor in our English language. Apparently, Truman rejected two-handed economists whose hands were tied, even as they served him hand and foot. Talk about a left-handed compliment. You really have to hand it to Mr. Truman.

Now open this small handbook, a manual of manual words and expressions that leave our language anything but shorthanded. Some words with *hand* in them go hand in glove with handedness while others, such as *handsome* (which originally meant *"easy to handle"*), are more opaque. In the seventeenth century, people played a betting game that involved the passing of betting money by hand into a cap held by an umpire. The game came to be called *hand i' cap* ("hand in cap"), whence our word *handicap*.

Many of our common words play right into our hands by deriving from *manus*, the Latin word for "hand": *manacle, maneuver, manicure, manipulate, manual, manufacture, manumit, manuscript,* and *emancipate*, "to remove one's hands from."

Ambidextrous, from Latin roots meaning "using both the left and right hands with equal ease," is a twelve-letter word in which the first six letters—*ambide*—are drawn from the left-hand side of the alphabet and the second six letters—*xtrous*—are from the right side. The opposite of *ambidextrous* is *ambisinister*: "clumsy, as if possessing two left hands."

The hand figures in many of our common folk sayings: *A bird in the hand is worth two in the bush. Many hands make light work. The hand that rocks the cradle rules the world. Idle hands are the devil's workshop.*

All hands on deck! Hands reach out from many of our most intriguing expressions:

Caught red-handed means caught with blood on one's hands.

To win hands down refers to jockeys who have a comfortable lead in a race. They don't need to lift their hands to urge their horse forward, so they let their hands drop.

Handy-Dandy English

Hand over fist was originally a seafaring term referring to the hand-over-hand movements made by an old hand during rapid ascent into the rigging of a sailing ship.

To wash one's hands of the matter alludes to Pontius Pilate's action, as described in the Gospel of Matthew, of washing his hands before the riotous crowd, symbolizing that Christ's death was out of his hands.

The history of the *shaking hands,* traditionally done with the right hand, reaches back to the fifth century B.C. in Greece. The friendly greeting was proof that the other person and you came in peace and were not going to take out a sword or other weapon to fight each other. In the words of Indira Gandhi, "You cannot shake hands with a clenched fist."

We can put our finger on *prestidigitator.* As impressive as that word looks and sounds, its derivation is quite simple. In 1843, Jules de Robére coined the word from the Italian *presto,* "quick," and the Latin *digitus,* "finger." A prestidigitator radiates the illusion of possessing magical powers through skill with his or her quick hands. *Chiropractic* is fashioned from two Greek roots that mean "done by hand, put into practice."

Have you heard about the woman who married Mr. Right but soon found out that his middle name was *Always*?

Right started out in life as an adjective that meant "straight, lawful, true, genuine, just, good, fair, proper, and fitting." Only later did *right* come to signify the right hand or right side. Ever since, *right* suggests rectitude, to which it is etymologically related: "You are in the right about this issue." "Throckmorton is the boss's right-hand man." "Her left hand doesn't know what the right one is doing."

The bias toward the right side extends beyond English. One who is skilled is *dexterous,* from the Latin *dexter,* meaning "right, on the right hand," and *adroit,* from the French *a droit,* "to the right."

On the other hand—the left one, of course—language appears to libel the left-handed: "That sounds like a left-handed compliment to me." "When it comes to grammar, I'm out in left field." "On the dance floor, Taylor seems to have two left feet."

Bias against the left-handed minority is embedded in many languages. *Sinister*, the Latin for "left, on the left hand," yields the darkly threatening *sinister* in English, while the French word for "left hand" is *gauche*, the debasement of which is *gawky*. Apparently, it is not only doorknobs, school desks, athletic gear, musical instruments, can openers, and flush handles on toilets that favor the right-handed majority.

Thumbs up for thumbs!

Finger entered our language through a very old Germanic root that means "one in five." "Hold on," you might object. "The thumb is not a finger, so a finger can't be one in five." I beg to differ. The Old English ancestor to *thumb, thuma,* meant "swollen finger."

I never *thumb my nose* at thumb expressions. To thumb one's nose, also known as *cocking a snook*, is a sign of disrespect fashioned by placing the thumb on one's nose, keeping the palm open, and wiggling the four remaining fingers.

Tom Thumb, the hero of many folktales, is so called because he is the size of his father's thumb.

Despite what you may read on the internet, the phrase *rule of thumb* has nothing to do with an antique British law enjoining a husband from using a stick thicker than his thumb to beat his wife. What a horrible thought! That law would stick out like a sore thumb!

Rule of thumb actually began back in the days when rulers of the measuring kind were uncommon, and woodworkers used the length of the thumb from the knuckle to the tip as an approximate measure of one inch—inexact, but better than nothing. Nowadays, *rule of thumb* signifies any rough-and-ready method of estimating, keeping one's fingers crossed that the rule will work.

The Tooth, the Whole Tooth, and Nothing But the Tooth

What did the Buddhist say in the dentist chair? *"No Novocain, please. I always transcend dental medication."*

Have you heard about the dentist and manicurist who got married? *Their union didn't last long because they lived hand to mouth and fought tooth and nail.*

What do you call a dentist's office? *A filling station.*

Why do dentists seem moody? *Because they're always looking down in the mouth.*

A number of dentists will tell you that getting me to sit still in a dentist's chair is like pulling teeth. Nonetheless, the oral metaphors in our language provide a topic that I can really sink my teeth into and go over with a fine-tooth comb.

You might think that expressions about our choppers, grinders, ivories, and pearly whites would be as scarce as hens' teeth. (Hens, of course, don't have any teeth.) But you don't have to give your eyeteeth to come up with a lot of toothsome examples.

The eyeteeth are so called because they are located directly below the eyes in the upper jaw. They are also called canine teeth because they resemble the pointed teeth of dogs. As such, they are especially useful in holding and tearing meat. Because they have long roots, eyeteeth can be the most difficult and painful of teeth to extract. Thus, if you would *give your eyeteeth*, you are willing to go through a lot to acquire something.

The English used to call a yellow-flowered weed a "lion's tooth" because the jagged, pointed leaves resembled the lion's snarly grin. During the early fourth century, the lion's-tooth plant took on a French flavor and became the *dent-de-lion,* "tooth-of-the-lion." Then it reacquired an English accent: *dandelion.*

Teeth are often cited to indicate strength. We talk about an agreement that *has teeth in it.* We describe strong winds and sarcastic comments as *biting.* When a fighter is in the *teeth of battle, fighting tooth and nail* (biting and scratching) and *armed to the teeth,* he's carrying all the weapons he can on his person, so the only place to put the last one is between his teeth.

We call some women *toothsome,* not because they possess prominent teeth, but because their appearance is pleasing to the palate of the eyes.

Not surprisingly, teeth are associated with matters culinary. In parts of our country, Italian sandwiches are called *grinders* because it takes a good set of teeth to eat them. Pasta should be cooked *al dente,* "to the tooth," in other words, cooked just enough to retain a somewhat firm texture for the teeth. Spanish cookbooks call for using a *diente* from a *cabeza* of garlic—that is, a "tooth" from a "head" of garlic.

Teeth are also associated with duplicity. We talk about people who *lie through their teeth,* that is, who force themselves to assume a calm demeanor that will conceal their true feelings. They display a hearty smile, baring and clenching their teeth as a means of controlling their emotions and pretending that butter wouldn't melt in their mouths. Closely related is the expression *to laugh out of the wrong side of your mouth,* which originally meant "to laugh in a forced way," perhaps by opening only one corner of your mouth. "Which side of the mouth is the wrong side?" we wonder.

Many phrases from the Book of Job in the Old Testament have become proverbial in our language: "Naked came I from my mother's womb, and naked shall I return"; "The Lord gave, and the Lord hath taken away"; and "My bone cleaveth to my skin and to my flesh, and I am escaped with the skin of my teeth." This last phrase has been altered slightly to "by the skin of my teeth."

Despite objections that the teeth don't have any skin, centuries of Bible reading have given the expression a permanent place in our language as a description of a close escape. Many interpret the skin in "skin of my teeth" to refer to the surface enamel covering the teeth, a film as thin as Job's margin of safety.

As with *dandelion,* animals and teeth converge in *mastodon,* the name we assign to those lumbering pre-elephants. *Mastodon* is composed of the Greek *mastos,* "breast," (as in *mastectomy*) and *odont,* "tooth," as in *orthodontia* ("correct teeth"). Mastodons are so named for the nipple-like protuberances on their molars. Rats, mice, squirrels, chipmunks, and beavers also get their name, *Rodentia,* from their teeth. Given these creatures' need to chew, chew, chew, because their teeth never stop growing, it's no mystery that they get their family name from the verb "to gnaw."

Our twelve molars do the job of grinding up our food before it is swallowed and digested. It's no mystery, then, that *molar* descends from the Latin *molaris,* "grinding tooth," but it may surprise you that the ancients named the tooth after *mola,* "a millstone."

The space I've left at the start of each paragraph is an *indentation.* When we indent a paragraph (from the Latin *dens,* "tooth," by way of the French *dent*), we take a chunk, or small bite, out of the beginning. *Indenture,* from the same root, strictly means "a document with serrated edges," referring to the once-common practice of cutting contracts into halves with jagged edges—one half for each party to the agreement. By fitting the edges together, one could authenticate the document.

A trident is a three-pronged spear that exhibits three "teeth." In Greek mythology, the god Poseidon brandished a trident to rule over the sea.

When we describe a golden-ager as *long in the tooth,* we are reflecting the fact that our gums recede with age, thereby displaying more and more roots. It is the same with horses. The age and health of a horse can be ascertained by examining the condition and number of its teeth. Although an animal may appear young and frisky, a close inspection may reveal that it is "long in the tooth" and ready for the glue factory.

Still, it is considered bad manners to inspect the teeth of a horse that has been given to you and, by extension, to inquire too closely into the value of any gift. Now you know the origin of *Don't look a gift horse in the mouth,* one of our oldest proverbs, whinnying back at least fifteen hundred years.

On the other hoof, if you decide to pay money to a horse trader, you are advised to determine whether the horse is a young stud or an old nag by examining the teeth and obtaining your information *straight from the horse's mouth,* precisely where responsible word searchers should look.

Your dentist may recommend that you gargle, and perhaps you have noticed that *gargle* and *gargoyle* exude similar sounds. Turns out that the two words are related because of the gargling sound made by cathedral waterspout heads. Both *gargoyle* and *gargle* derive from the Old French *gargouille,* meaning "throat, waterspout," apparently from the water passing through the mouths of the grotesque figures.

Words From the Heart

In the English language, the heart is often used to denote the seat of passion, compassion, courage, and intelligence. Of all the parts of the body, the heart is the one that pulses most pervasively through our daily conversation. As the song from *Damn Yankees* proclaims, "You Gotta Have Heart!"

If, for example, you are deeply saddened, you might say that you are *heartsick, heartbroken, downhearted, heavy-hearted,* or *discouraged.* At the heart of *discouraged* beats the Latin *cor,* "heart," giving the word the literal meaning of *disheartened.* Additional progeny of *cor* include *accord, concord, discord, record, cordial,* and *cardiac.*

If you wish to emphasize your sincerity, you might say *heartfelt, with all my heart, from the bottom of my heart,* or *in my heart of hearts.*

If something pleases you greatly, that something is to your *heart's delight* or *it warms the cockles of your heart.* A cockle is a bivalve mollusk of the genus *Cardium* (Latin "heart") that takes its name from its shape, which resembles that of a human heart.

It was once the custom for a young man to attach to his sleeve a gift, such as a scarf, from his sweetheart or to wear her name embroidered on his sleeve, thus displaying his feelings for the world to see. Seizing on this practice, William Shakespeare, in his tragedy *Othello,* gave the world the expression *to wear your heart on your sleeve,* meaning "to show your emotions."

Heart is also a letter-playful word. Loop the *h* from the front to the back and, behold, *earth.* Or simply add an *h* to the end of *heart* and get *hearth,* the heart of the home.

Using the definitions that follow, identify each common word or expression that contains the word *heart*.

1. to take seriously 2. please be merciful 3. beloved person 4. be reassured 5. desire earnestly
6. frightened 7. discouraged 8. incomplete, as in an effort 9. complete, as in an effort 10. substantial, as a meal
11. mental anguish 12. the central issue 13. brave, courageous 14. cowardly 15. uninvolved
16. swear to tell the truth 17. characterizing a good person 18. characterizing a cruel person 19. an especially attractive man 20. give up
21. regret deeply and painfully 22. one who shows extravagant sympathy 23. memorize 24. indigestion 25. play hard
26. just what you like 27. a change in how you feel 28. reassure 29. the essential emotion, as of a nation 30. youthful in attitude
31. very sad 32. characterizing an intimate conversation 33. thoroughly evil 34. cheerful, free from anxiety 35. suspenseful
36. you show empathy 37. be well-intentioned 38. deeply satisfying 39. strive mightily 40. intimately connected

Answers

1. take to heart 2. have a heart 3. sweetheart, heart of my heart 4. take heart 5. have your heart set on
6. have your heart in your mouth 7. disheartened 8. half-hearted 9. whole-hearted 10. hearty
11. heartache 12. the heart of the matter, at the heart of 13. lion-hearted 14. faint of heart, chickenhearted 15. your heart isn't in it
16. cross your heart 17. heart of gold, good-hearted 18. heartless, heart of stone, hardhearted 19. heartthrob 20. lose heart
21. eat your heart out 22. a bleeding heart 23. learn by heart 24. heartburn 25. play your heart out

26. after your own heart 27. a change of heart 28. put someone's heart at rest 29. the heartbeat 30. young at heart

31. heartrending 32. heart-to-heart 33. black-hearted 34. light-hearted 35. heart-stopping

36. your heart goes out to 37. have your heart in the right place 38. to your heart's content 39. put your heart into it 40. close to your heart

Body of Knowledge

One of the amazements of language is that it seeks to name everything. Now that you've learned about four familiar body parts, listen to an organ recital of lesser-known components of the human chassis:

- *acnestis.* The part of your back between your shoulder blades that you can't quite reach to scratch
- *canthus.* The point at either end of each eye where your upper and lower lids meet
- *frenulum.* The membrane that attaches your tongue to the floor of your mouth
- *glabella.* The smooth space between your eyebrows
- *hallux.* Your big toe. The little toe is called the *minimus*
- *intergluteal cleft.* the crease between the two large gluteal muscles you sit on, or, less technically, your butt crack
- *opisthenar.* The back of the hand, opposite your palm
- *philtrum.* The cleft that runs from just below your nose to the middle of your upper lip
- *popliteal.* The hollow area at the back of your knee
- *puncta.* The tiny openings on the margins of your eyelids. About the size of a grain of rice, these tiny plugs stop fluid from draining from the eye, help keep the eye's surface moist and comfortable, and relieve itching, burning, red eyes.
- *purlicue.* The web of flesh between your thumb and forefinger
- *rasceta.* The horizontal creases on the inside of your wrists

- *suprasternal notch.* The depression below your neck between your clavicles
- *thenar.* The fleshy pad on your palm just below your thumb
- *tragus.* The fleshy bump of the ear between the side of your face and your ear cavity
- *uvula.* The ball that hangs down from the back of your throat
- *vomer.* The slender bone that separates your nostrils

😀Crazy English

English is a crazy language. You drive in a parkway and park in a driveway, and your nose can run and your feet can smell. Because we speakers and writers of English seem to have our heads screwed on backwards and our heads up our you-know-whats, we constantly misperceive our bodies:

- *Watch your head.* I keep seeing this sign on low doorways, but I haven't figured out how to follow the instructions. Trying to watch your head is like trying to bite your teeth.
- *They're head over heels in love.* That's nice, but all of us do almost everything *head over heels*. If we are trying to create an image of people doing cartwheels and somersaults, why don't we say, "They're heels over head in love"?
- When we yell, *Heads up!* don't we really mean *Heads down!*
- If *fatty* means "full of fat," shouldn't *skinny* mean "full of skin"?
- *The athlete never left her feet.* Of course not! Her feet are attached to her ankles.
- *His feet are firmly planted on the ground.* Then how can he get his pants on and off?
- *He's got a good head on his shoulders.* What? He doesn't have a neck?
- *She broke every bone in her body.* What about the bones outside her body?
- *Put your best foot forward.* Now let's see… We have a good foot and a better foot—but we don't have a third—and best—foot. It's our better foot we want to put forward.

- *Keep a stiff upper lip.* When we are disappointed or afraid, which lip do we try to control? The lower lip, of course, is the one we are trying to keep from quivering.
- *I'm speaking tongue in cheek.* So how can anyone understand you? (Back in the eighteenth century, people would puff out their cheeks with their tongue to indicate they were speaking in jest, kind of like a sly wink today. Similarly, *to bite one's tongue* meant "to suppress having to laugh out loud.")
- *They do things behind my back.* You want they should do things in front of your back?
- *They did it ass backwards.* What's wrong with that? We do *everything* ass backwards.

THAT'S ENTERTAINMENT!

Face the Music

William Shakespeare began his comedy *Twelfth Night* with the line "If music be the food of love, play on!" About a century later, the playwright William Congreve opened his comedy *The Mourning Bride* with the equally famous line "Music has charms to soothe a savage breast" (almost always misquoted as "the savage beast").

If music be the food of love, it is also the food of language. Music has charms that teem our tongues, course through our pens, and stream from our keyboards.

I am often asked to be a keynote speaker. I don't speak to trumpet my accomplishments, blow my own horn, or drum up business for my books. Rather, I come to set the proper key and the proper note and to strike a responsive chord. A keynote speaker delivers a keynote address in which he or she develops the underlying theme of a gathering. The term *keynote* began with the practice of playing a note before a group, such as a barbershop quartet, started singing a cappella. The note sounded determined the key in which the song would be performed; thus, the term *keynote*.

Keynote is one word in a symphony of musical metaphors that sing throughout our everyday vocabulary. Aria ready to face the music? Of chorus you are. Many actors experience a touch of stage fright at the moment of going onstage. But, looking out across the orchestra pit, each performer must *face the music*, as I now ask you to do.

You may feel that there's too much sax and violins in my writing. You may think me a Johnny-one-note who's preaching to the choir and doesn't know his brass from his oboe. But all I can say to that is

"Fiddlesticks! I've got an upbeat attitude. I'm feeling fit as a fiddle, and I don't fiddle around or play second fiddle to anybody."

I'm a one-man band, and I march to the beat of a different drummer. I'm not going to give you a second-string performance or play it by ear or harp on the subject. Rather, I'm an unsung hero who's going to pull out all the stops and not soft-pedal any aspect of our melodious, mellifluous English language.

Second-string originally meant a set of violin strings kept on hand in case the strings in the instrument broke. When we talk or write about someone *soft-pedaling* something, we are referring to the soft pedal on a piano that is used to modify the timbre. When we soft-pedal an idea, we moderate and play it down. If, on the other hand, we do the opposite and *pull out all the stops*, we are like an organist who pulls out all the knobs (stops) in the organ to bring all the pipes into play.

To harp on, meaning "to dwell on the same topic," is a shortening of the old phrase *to harp on one string,* which meant "to play one note on a harp string over and over." A student once wrote, "In the Bible, David was a Hebrew king skilled at playing the liar." The budding scholar meant *lyre,* a harp-like instrument played by the ancient Greeks. *Lyre* bequeaths us the words *lyric* and *lyrical.*

Show me a piano falling down a mineshaft, and I'll show you A flat minor.

I, your unsung hero, will now waltz out of here without missing a beat—not on a sour note but on a high note. Please remember that I'm not just whistling Dixie, and I don't mean to chime in and harp on this subject to beat the band. Sure, I'm all keyed up and jazzed up, but I'm not here to give you a song and dance or create a cheap soap opera that draws a chorus of boos. In this book, nobody has to pay the piper.

Rather, I'm trying to steal the show and orchestrate an overture so that we can ring in a harmonious relationship, get in tune with each other, and hop on the same bandwagon. Then you'll sing a different tune, and we can make beautiful music together.

Show Biz in the Limelight

Because entertainment is such a joyful, enriching part of our world, show business metaphors help our language to *get its act together* and *get the show on the road*. At the opportune moment, these sprightly words and expressions stop *waiting in the wings* and *step out into the limelight*. After all, *the show must go on*.

The first limelights were theatrical spotlights that used heated calcium oxide, or quicklime, to give off a light that was brilliant and white but not hot. Ever since that bright idea, *to be in the limelight* has been a metaphor for being in the glare of public scrutiny. Such show biz metaphors become *a tough act to follow*.

Break a leg is a cliché well-wishers say ironically to actors, singers, and musicians before they go on stage to perform. The origin of the imperative is obscure. One theory shifts the meaning of the word *break*, claiming that the expression means "May you take so many bows that the line of your leg will break multiply at the knee as the audience continues to applaud." This interpretation is supported by the expression *make a leg*, "to make a deep bow with the right leg drawn back," which started in the late sixteenth century.

Slapstick comedy owes its name to the double lath that clowns in seventeenth-century pantomimes wielded. The terrific sound of the two flat wooden sticks slapping together on the harlequin's derriere banged out the word *slapstick*.

One of the puppet clowns who did the slapping was Punch, forever linked to his straightwoman Judy. The Punch that is so pleased in the cliché *pleased as Punch* is not the sweet stuff we quaff. That phrase, in fact, alludes to the cheerful singing and self-satisfaction of the manic puppet Punch.

From the art of puppetry we gain another expression. Puppet masters manipulate the strings of their marionettes from behind a dark curtain. Unseen, they completely control the actions of their on-stage actors. Whence the expression *to pull strings*.

For my closing act, I shine the spotlight on a few show-stopping words that were born backstage and onstage:

Claptrap was originally a theatrical trick designed to attract (*trap*) applause (*clap*) in a theater. It might have been a showy line, such as "Britannia rules the waves!" Thus, *claptrap* compares a clap trapper to a shallow, showy, cheap sentiment expressed solely for effect.

Playwrights, novelists, screenwriters, and other storytellers involve their characters in a plot in which they become tied in a knot woven from the complicated threads of the storyline. The *denouement*, from the French *desnouer*, "to untie," is the outcome of the plot complications that have bound the characters.

Desultory jumps down from the Latin *de-*, "from," and *salire*, "to leap." The Roman *desultors*, or leapers, were circus performers who performed the feat of jumping from one galloping horse to another. They were soon compared with people who fitfully jumped from one idea to another in conversation or one goal to another in their lives.

Explode comes from the Latin *explodere*, "to chase away by clapping one's hands." In ancient Rome, audiences were terrifically active in expressing their praise or disapproval of actors. Disgruntled theatergoers would clap loudly to show their dissatisfaction with the performance on stage. (To show approval, ancient Romans would wave the flap of their togas.)

Hanky-panky is possibly created, with the aid of reduplication, from the magician's handkerchief, or "hanky," a prop for trickery and sleight of hand. Or *hanky-panky* may be an alteration of *hocus-pocus*.

Hypocrite is an offspring of the Greek *hypokrites,* a stage actor who, by the nature of his occupation, often wore a mask and pretended to be someone other than himself. By extension, a hypocrite pretends to beliefs or feelings he doesn't really have.

Person also steps from the stage into our everyday parlance. In Greek and Roman theater, actors played more than one role during a performance simply by donning a *persona* ("mask") to change character. Eventually, *persona* came to mean the role an individual assumes in life and, later, the individual himself.

The ancient Athenian playwright, producer, and stage director Thespis is often dubbed the Father of Greek Tragedy. Until his time, dramatic presentations in Greece consisted entirely of singing by a chorus. Thespis is said to have innovated, in 534 B.C., the connection of the chorus directly to the plot and the role of the very first actor by having a member of the chorus step forward and carry on a dialogue with the other members. We remember his name in the word *thespian,* "actor."

You're a real trouper to have stayed with this lesson in etymology to the final curtain call. Note that the spelling isn't the military *trooper,* but *trouper,* a member of a theater company. *A real trouper* now means "one who perseveres through hardship without complaint."

On with the show!

A Circus of Words

When you say or write *a three-ring circus*, you are actually repeating yourself because *circus* echoes *kirkos*, the Greek word for "ring, circle." In 2017, after 146 years of bedazzling Americans from California to the New York island, the Ringling Bros. and Barnum & Bailey Circus folded its tents. Pulled by dwindling attendance and mounting operating costs, the final curtain came down on the Greatest Show on Earth:

> Nothing now to mark the spot
>   But a littered vacant lot.
> Sawdust in a heap, and where
>   The center ring stood, grass worn bare.
>
> But remain the sounds and sights—
>   The artists, music, beasts, and lights.
> May the spangled memories soar
>   In our hearts forevermore.

But a number of smaller circuses endure, and their special vocabulary stays alive. Communities are most likely to develop a colorful argot when they have limited contact with the world outside of their group. The circus community is a perfect example of the almost monastic self-containment in which argot flourishes. Big top people travel in very close quarters, and because they usually go into a town, set up, do a show, tear down, and leave, they have little contact with the locals. They socialize with each other, they intermarry, and their children acquire the argot from the time they start to talk.

"Hey, First-of-May! Tell the butcher in the back yard to stay away from the bulls, humps, stripes, and painted ponies. We have some cherry pie for him before doors and spec." Sound like doubletalk? Actually, that's circus talk—or, more technically, circus argot, argot being a specialized vocabulary used by a particular group for mutual bonding and private communication.

First-of-May designates anyone who is brand-new to circus work. That's because circuses used to start their tours around the first day in May. A *candy butcher* is a concessionaire who sells cotton candy (*floss*) and other food, along with drinks and souvenirs, to the audience during the show. The *backyard* is the place just behind the circus entrance where performers wait to do their acts. A *bull* is a circus elephant, even though most of them are female. Among other circus beasts, *humps, stripes,* and *painted ponies* are, respectively, camels, tigers, and zebras. *Cherry pie* is extra work, probably from *chairy pie,* the setting up of extra chairs around the arena. *Doors!* is the cry that tells circus folk that the audience is coming in to take their seats, and *spec* is short for *spectacle,* the big parade of all the performers.

Trust me: This topic ain't no *dog and pony show*—the designation for a small circus with just a few acts, also known as a *mud show.*

What we call the toilet circus folk call the *donniker,* the hot dog or grill concession trailer where the circus people can snag a snack is a *grease joint,* and a circus performer is a *kinker.* The townspeople are *towners* or *rubes.* In the old days, when large groups of towners who believed (sometimes accurately) that they had been fleeced by dishonest circus people, they would come back in a mob to seek retribution. The cry *Hey rube!* went out, and everyone knew that the fight was on.

When a circus came to town, the sheriff would often remove the nut from a wheel of the main wagon. Because in bygone days these nuts were elaborately and individually crafted, they were well-nigh impossible to replace. Thus, the circus couldn't leave town until the costs of land, utilities, rental, easements, and security were paid. It's but a short metaphorical leap to the modern meaning of *making the nut,* "meeting one's expenses."

Close, but no cigar is a twentieth-century American phrase that alludes to the workers in circus and carnival booths who awarded cigars as prizes. The expression applied to those who were close to winning a prize, but failed to do so; that is, "just short of being perfect."

A full house is called a *straw house,* from the days when straw would be laid down in front of the seats to accommodate more people than the seats could hold. Distances between engagements were called *jumps.* Thus, an old circus toast rings out: "May your lots be grassy, your jumps short, and your houses straw."

Ladies and gentlemen! Children of all ages! For my closing act, I present two stories:

At the end of the nineteenth century, a crisis arose in the Barnum and Bailey Circus. The man who was shot out of the cannon every day was asked by his wife to quit his high-risk profession, much to the distress of Phineas Taylor Barnum, "the Greatest Showman on Earth." P.T., whose wit was equal to his showmanship, summoned the fellow and said, "I beg you to reconsider. Men of your caliber are hard to find." Barnum, of course, was perpetrating a playful pun on the word *caliber,* which, from its earliest beginnings, meant "the diameter of a bullet or other projectile."

Egress, from the Latin *e,* "out" + *gress,* "step," is a fancy word for *exit,* and P. T. Barnum, made creative use of it. Barnum's American Museum in Lower Manhattan was so popular that it attracted up to fifteen thousand customers daily, and some would spend the entire day there. This cut into profits, as the museum would be too full to squeeze another person in. In classic Barnum style, P. T. put up above a cage holding a mother tiger and her cubs a sign that read, TIGRESS. Then, over a doorway next to that sign, he put up another sign that said, TO THE EGRESS. Many customers followed that sign, looking for an exhibit featuring an exotic female bird. What they found instead was themselves out the door ("the Egress") and back on the street. Once they had exited the building, the door would lock behind them, and if they wanted to get back in, they had to pay another admission charge.

☺Ana Gram the Juggler

Can you create one word out of the letters in *new door*?

The answer (bwa ha ha) is *one word*. The letters in *new door* are the same as those in *one word*, except in a different order.

When is enough not enough?

When you rearrange the letters in *enough*, you get *one hug*. Everybody knows that one hug is never enough!

Read this little verse, noting the italicized words, and answer the question "What am I?":

On my top a twisted *thorn*.
On my right a broken *seat*.
Below me sits a shattered *shout*,
And on my left a well-stirred *stew*.

The answer is: I am a compass. *Thorn, seat, shout,* and *stew* anagram into *north, east, south,* and *west*.

These three riddles involve anagrams. An anagram is a rearrangement of all the letters in a familiar word, phrase, or name to form another word, phrase, or name.

To introduce you to the more spectacular examples of alphabetic manipulation, I present the greatest juggler in the world, the very art and soul of the word circus—Ana Gram! She can twirl balls, clubs, plates, hoops, or flaming torches; but she's best when she's spinning letters.

Ladies and Gentlemen! Boys and girls! Children of all ages! Don't *waddle*! Don't *dawdle*! It's time for Anagramarama! It's *tedious outside*, so stay inside and enjoy the fun *residing* at *ringside*, where you will see a *genuine ingénue*, the high *priest* of *esprit*, and *ripest sprite* of letter play of the highest *stripe*. Speaking of "letter play of the highest stripe," here's a *mite* of an *item* that at no *time* will make you *emit groans* from your *organs*. Gaze upon a poem that contains nine anagrams of the same eight letters:

Arty Idol

Watch Ana Gram, and you will see
Her act inspires *idolatry*.
Please do not come *o tardily*,
And *dilatory* please don't be.

Adroitly Ana Gram will start
To alter *daily rot*. She's smart.
A *dirty lot*, an *oily dart*
She'll change into the *doily art*.

I *enlist* you to be *silent* and *listen* to the *inlets* of my *tinsel* words. As we *begin* our *binge* of letter juggling, *please* don't fall *asleep*, or your *retina* will not *retain* the *overt trove* of *laudatory*, *adulatory* letter wizardry, which has for too long *continued unnoticed*.

Simple logic *impels* your positive *reactions* to Ana Gram's creations. Among *robust turbos*, she's an absolute *dynamo*, even on a *Monday*—a *gagster* who will *stagger* you with her *latent talent*. She's the *antagonist* of *stagnation*, the *flauntress* of *artfulness*, and a *patroness* who can *transpose* a *sword* into *words* that *float aloft*. Each *emphatic*, *empathic*, *seraph phrase* will *reclaim* the *miracle* of language.

Her *stagery gyrates* the *grayest* spirit. Before you *reunite* with your *retinue* or retreat through the *ingress,* please attend to this greatest of *singers,* a *singer* who *reigns* and who will never *resign* as our *merriest rimester.* She's one of those crowd-*pleaser leapers* whose *dances ascend* to the *highest heights.* No *dictionary* is *indicatory* of the *elation* you will experience down to your very *toenail,* a joy that will *roost* in the *roots* of your *torso.*

She's the very *heart* of the *earth,* a *damsel* who's won many *medals.* With a *lovely volley* of letters, she juggles a *cheap peach,* an *Argentine tangerine,* and *solemn lemons* and *melons.* At the same time, she *reaps, pares,* and then manages to *spear pears,* while twirling *pastel plates* (a *staple* of her act) and balancing a *maraschino* cherry on her nose as she plays two *harmonicas.*

Lucky ladies and gentlemen! *Cripes!* Just think of the low *prices* we offer:

DISCOUNTER INTRODUCES REDUCTIONS

Look closely at the *poster,* and *presto! boing! bingo!* you'll see an *integral alerting, altering, relating triangle.* What you see is a trianagram [three ten-letter words, each a rearrangement of the other two]. Now I, your circus pitchman, will be busy *mastering emigrants streaming* [a nine-letter trianagram] into the tent. I hope that someone will have *cautioned* them not to have *auctioned* off their *education* [yet another nine-letter trianagram]. That could lead to *intercoastal altercations* [twelve-letter anagram!]

The *charisma* of Ana's performance *is a charm.* In her *persistent prettiness,* you *observe* the *obverse* of the *verbose. Pleased* by what has *elapsed* and astounded by such *climaxes,* everyone *exclaims* that it would be impossible to *reproduce* her *procedure* to *intoxicate* your *excitation.* She never *mutilates* songs. She'll only *stimulate ultimates.* She will not *enervate* you, and you will *venerate* her. She'll *edify,* and you'll *deify* the *luster* of the *result* she'll *rustle* up.

☺ THE PALINDROMEDARY

A palindrome, from two Greek roots that mean "to run forward and backward," is a word or statement that reads the same forward and backward. Even if you're a dud, kook, boob, or poop, palindromes should make you exult, "Ah ha!, Oh, ho!, Hey, yeh!, Yo boy!, Yay!, Wow!"

Here's an exclusive interview I conducted with the Palindromedary himself, the two-way statement made flesh. This camel is a talking animal smitten with Ailihphilia—the love of palindromes. Everything the Palindromedary says is a WORD ROW. YA, WOW! TWO-WAY WORD ROW that reads both ways.

LEDERER: So you're the famous Palindromedary.
PALINDROMEDARY: I, MALE, MACHO, OH, CAMEL AM I.

I see that, despite your fame, you're wearing a name tag. Why?
GATEMAN SEES NAME. GARAGEMAN SEES NAME TAG.

Is it true that you were discovered in the Nile region?
CAMEL IN NILE, MAC.

I heard that the trainer said an earful to the flying elephant in your menagerie. What was the trainer's command?
"DUMBO, LOB MUD."

I hear Dan, the lion tamer, is sick in bed.
POOR DAN IS IN A DROOP.

Richard Lederer

Is anybody treating Dan?
   DR. AWKWARD.

So there won't be a lion performance today?
   NO, SIT! CAT ACT IS ON.

What was the last act you saw?
   OH WHO WAS IT I SAW, OH WHO?

Well, have you seen the big cats in action?
   WAS IT A CAR OR A CAT I SAW?

Why won't we be witnessing the performing dog?
   A DOG? A PANIC IN A PAGODA!

Where do you keep the dogs?
   POOCH COOP.

I heard that somebody slipped something into the dog cage.
   GOD! A RED NUGGET! A FAT EGG UNDER A DOG!

The menagerie includes gnus. Did those gnus actually sing the *Star Spangled Banner*?
   RISE, NUT! GNUS SUNG TUNE, SIR.

What about the rumor that one of the gnus is ill?
   UNGASTROPERITONITIS—IS IT I? NOT I, REPORTS A GNU.

What's the problem when you come after the gnu act?
   GNU DUNG.

What happened when you followed the dog act?
   DID I STEP ON DOG DOO? GOOD GOD! NO PETS! I DID!

The Palindromedary

Why aren't the owls performing tonight?
   TOO HOT TO HOOT.

And the panda?
   PANDA HAD NAP.

And the elk?
   ELK CACKLE.

And the rat?
   OOZY RAT IN A SANITARY ZOO.

And the deer?
   DEER FRISK, SIR, FREED.

Did you see Kay and her yak?
   KAY, A RED NUDE, PEEPED UNDER A YAK.

Is it also true that you sewed a dress for the kangaroo?
   I MADE KANGAROO TUTU. TOO RAG-NAKED AM I.

What's one of your favorite human circus acts?
   TRAPEZE PART.

And what's especially exciting about the trapeze?
   TEN ON TRAPEZE PART! NO NET!

No net?
   NO TENT NET ON.

You seem truly excited about the circus.
   AVID AS A DIVA.

Are there any acts that you would get rid of?
   DUDE, NOT ONE DUD.

But what do you say to those who contend that the circus can't survive as an art form?

"NO! IT CAN! ACTION!"

Mr. Palindromedary, we thank you for such a scintillating two-way interview. Is it true that you are the only animal who can speak intelligibly in palindromes?

YES, THAT'S TRUE. ALL OTHER ANIMALS SAY THINGS LIKE *"EKILS GNIH TYASS LAMINAR EHTOLLAE URTSTAHT SEY."*

My Kids, the Poker Players

As luck would have it, you're reading a book written by one of the most successful breeders of world-class poker professionals ever. My son, Howard "The Professor" Lederer, and daughter, Annie "The Duchess of Poker" Duke, have taken home eleven and a half million dollars in poker championships. They are the first sibling pair to have reached the final table of a World Series of Poker event, and both have won WSOP bracelets.

My children's achievements in the gaming halls inspire me to deal from a full deck of vivid words and phrases that have made the journey from the poker table into our everyday conversation and writing. The colorful and high-risk excitement of poker have made the language of the game among the most pervasive metaphors in our everyday parlance.

The basic elements of poker are the cards, the chips, and the play of the hand. Each has become embedded in our daily parlance. Beginning with the cards, the verb *to discard* descends from *decard*, "away card," and first meant to throw away a card from one's hand. Gradually, the meaning of *discard* broadened to include rejection beyond card playing. A cardsharp who is out to cheat you may be dealing from the bottom of the deck and giving you a fast shuffle, in which case you may get lost in the shuffle.

You might call a low-down skunk *a four-flusher. Flush,* a hand of five cards of a single suit, flows from the Latin *fluxus,* "flow." A *four-flusher* characterizes a poker player who pretends to such good fortune but in fact holds a worthless hand of only four same-suit cards. If you don't know that a flush beats a straight, you will be flush-straighted at a poker table.

The cleverest application of poker terminology that I've encountered appears on the sides of some plumbing trucks: "A Flush Is Better Than a Full House." In poker that isn't true, but a homeowner would recognize its wisdom.

Now that I've laid my cards on the table, let's see what happens when the chips are down. Why do we call a gilt-edged, sure-thing stock *a blue-chip stock?* Because the blue chips have traditionally been the most valuable. Why, when we compare the value of two things, do we often ask how one *stacks up* against the other, as in "How do the Cardinals stack up against the Yankees?" Here the reference is to the columns of chips piled up before the players around a poker table. These stacks also account for the compound *bottom dollar. Betting one's bottom dollar* means wagering your entire stack right down to the felt. The metaphor of poker chips is so powerful that one of the euphemisms we use for death is *cashing in your chips.*

The guts of poker is the betting. *I'm all in,* risking your entire chip stack in one bet, has recently become a standard affirmative in American English, traveling from the game of No-Limit Texas Hold'em to our everyday vocabulary. If your opponents wish to call your bluff and insist that you put up or shut up, you'll be happy to put your money where your mouth is. Rather than passing the buck, maintain an inscrutable poker face, play it close to the vest, and hope to hit the jackpot.

Jackpot originally described the reward to the big winner in a game of progressive poker. In this game, you need a pair of jacks or better to "open the pot," and the stakes grow higher until the requisite pair is dealt. *Jackpot* has gradually expanded to include the pots of gold in slot machines, game shows, and state lotteries.

Pass the buck is a cliché that means "to shift responsibility," but why should handing someone a dollar indicate that a duty is transferred? Once again, the answer can be found in long-ago gambling pleasure palaces. The *buck* in *pass the buck* was originally a hunting knife whose handle was made from a buck's horn. The knife was

My Kids, the Poker Players

placed in front of the player to the left of the dealer who had to bet first, a position of liability. That knife gave the game its name—Buckhorn Poker or Buck Poker—and gave us the expression *pass the buck*. After each deal, the buck was passed from the first wagerer to the next player, changing the buck-passer's position from one of disadvantage to one of advantage.

In the Old West, silver dollars often replaced buckhorn knives as tokens, and these coins took on the slang name *buck*. President Harry S. Truman, reputed to be a skillful poker player, adopted the now-famous motto "The buck stops here," meaning that the ultimate responsibility rests with the president.

You can bet on it.

Most casinos house both poker games and dicing games. Dice roll across the felted table of our language. Many of us view life as a crapshoot, *craps* (a mispronunciation of the word *crabs*) being a game in which players bet on what numbers a pair of dice will reveal.

A *high roller* is a craps player who will roll the dice for big stakes. If that player experiences a lucky streak, he or she will be *on a roll*, meaning "unbeatable with the dice; very successful in one undertaking after another."

Make no bones about it, meaning "direct; uncomplaining," refers to the behavior of not yakking or complaining about the roll of the dice, or bones, as they are often called. *At sixes and sevens,* "all disorder and confusion," began in the old dice game of hazard, played with two dice, like craps, in which *sinque* and *sice* ("five" and "six") were the most risky bets to make. Anyone who tried to throw these numbers was considered careless and confused. Although the two words meant "five" and "six," they became *sixes and sevens,* a jocular shift to a total of the unlucky number thirteen.

In the card game of bridge, each team of two players tries to find out what suit is the best one in their combined hands. That's the story behind the two expressions that has traveled from bridge into our daily vocabulary—"to follow suit," which is required in bridge, unless your hand is "void" of that suit, and "[math] isn't my strong suit."

WE ALL SPEAK MOVIE LINES

Americans have fallen deeply in love with that beguiling conspiracy of light and darkness and color and silence and sound and music that we call the movies. In the movie theater and on smaller screens the boundaries between real and reel, the line between reality and movies, wavers and blurs. Something has happened to our American language—and we've a feeling we're not in Kansas anymore.

You probably recognize the second part of that statement as a borrowing from the iconic film *The Wizard of Oz*. Being transported out of Kansas is one of a passel of expressions from movies that have launched a thousand lips.

The first Academy Awards ceremony took place during a banquet held in the Blossom Room of the Hollywood Roosevelt Hotel. When the first awards were handed out on May 16, 1929, movies had just begun to talk. Two hundred and seventy attended, tickets cost ten dollars, and the awards part of the evening lasted fifteen minutes. I would love to have been a time traveler rushing into the Blossom Room to announce the luminous future of the movie industry.

So let's cut to the chase, an expression that refers to chase scenes in action movies. Early filmmakers made actual cuts and splices to the strips of film. A 1929 screenplay, for example, includes "Jannings escapes. Cut to chase." Ultimately, the idiom evolved from "enough of the kissy-kissy scene already; let's cut to the car chase" to a more figurative use: "Get to the point." That extended meaning is fairly recent, dating from only the early 1980s.

We All Speak Movie Lines

"Wait a minute! Wait a minute! You ain't heard nothin' yet!" That's what Al Jolson said in *The Jazz Singer* (1927), the mother of all talking films. Ever since, lines from the movies have shaped our hopes and dreams and aspirations and have suffused our everyday conversations.

Today I'm making you an offer you can't refuse—a version of the line in Mario Puzo's novel, *The Godfather* (1969) and the ensuing 1972 film.

So, "what's up, Doc?" That, of course, is Bugs Bunny's question to Elmer Fudd. What's up is that I hope never to hear from my readers, "What we got here is a failure to communicate" or "I'm mad as hell, and I'm not going to take this anymore!" The first statement began as Strother Martin's line in *Cool Hand Luke*, and the second is Peter Finch's furious protest in *Network*.

May you never sneer at me, "Frankly, my dear. I don't give a damn," spoken by Clark Gable in *Gone with the Wind*. Just remember that "tomorrow is another day," spoken by Vivien Leigh in the same film.

"I think this is the beginning of a beautiful friendship" is a line delivered by Humphrey Bogart in *Casablanca*. That film also bequeaths us "Round up the usual suspects," "Here's looking at you, kid," and the oft misquoted "Play it, Sam."

Read on, and "make my day"—the signature statement of the Clint Eastwood character Dirty Harry in the 1983 film *Sudden Impact*.

"Who you gonna call?"—your faithful language author! That's a snippet from *Ghostbusters*, and, of course, it should be "*whom* are you going to call?"

Now let's cut to the chase with a groovy movie game. Identify the movies whence come the following filmic expressions that inhabit our everyday conversations:

1. They're ba-a-a-ck! 2. If you build it, they will come. 3. Houston, we have a problem. 4. Greed is good. 5. You talkin' to me?

6. I coulda been a contender. 7. Why don't you come up and see me sometime? 8. Rosebud. 9. May the Force be with you! 10. Show me the money!

11. Love means never having to say you're sorry. 12. Heeeeere's Johnny! 13. There's no crying in baseball! 14. I'm the king of the world! 15. You're gonna need a bigger boat.

16. It was Beauty killed the Beast. 17. Win just one for the Gipper. 18. Who's on first. 19. They call me Mister Tibbs 20. I'll have what she's having.

21. E. T. phone home. 22. I love the smell of napalm in the morning. 23. Plastics. 24. Shaken, not stirred. 25. I want to be alone.

Answers

1. *Poltergeist* 2. *Field of Dreams* 3. *Apollo 13* 4. *Wall Street* 5. *Taxi Driver*

6. *On the Waterfront* 7. *She Done Him Wrong* 8. *Citizen Kane* 9. *Star Wars* 10. *Jerry Maguire*

11. *Love Story* 12. *The Shining* 13. *A League of Their Own* 14. *Titanic* 15. *Jaws*

16. *King Kong* 17. *Knute Rockne All-American* 18. *The Naughty Nineties* 19. *In the Heat of the Night* 20. *When Harry Met Sally*

21. *E. T. the Extra-Terrestrial* 22. *Apocalypse Now* 23. *The Graduate* 24. *Doctor No* 25. *Grand Hotel*

Finally, two lines that got their start in Merry Melodies and *Terminator 2: Judgment Day* —That's all, folks! Hasta la vista, baby!

Noah's Ark

BEASTLY WORD ORIGINS

The poet William Cowper wrote of

> philologists, who trace
> A panting syllable through time and space,
> Start it at home, and hunt it in the dark
> To Gaul, to Greece, and into Noah's ark.

The word *animal* is animated by the Latin *animalis*, "having breath or soul." We often refer to our fellow organisms that run and fly and swim and creep across the face of our planet as "dumb animals." It is true that these creatures do not speak in the human sense of that word, but they have made thousands of contributions to the power of human speech. To back up my claim, I have corralled a small herd of ungulates—herbivorous and hoofed mammals.

Buffalo buffalo buffalo Buffalo buffalo is a sentence that means that "buffalo from the city of Buffalo confuse other buffalo from the same city." That statement raises the question why *buffalo* (from a Latin word for "wild oxen") has become a verb denoting "to confuse, baffle, frustrate." The answer is that, despite the slaughter of tens of millions of American buffalo, the animal is hard to kill individually. Buffalo are swift, tough, and belligerent.

Products made from European buffalo hides have been plentiful for more than five hundred years, including strips of buffalo hide that were used to bring metals to a high polish. That's where we get the verb *to buff.* The vogue meaning of the adjective *buff* as "well built, muscular, hunky" further reflects the idea of "polished or made attractive."

In seventeenth-century Europe, certain soldiers wore coats made from buffalo hides. Because these buffcoats, as they were called, were the color of human skin, *in the buff* arose as a synonym for "naked."

In nineteenth-century America, firemen wore thick, sturdy coats made from buffalo hides as their winter gear. Dandies, who had nothing better to do than to rush to fires and watch the burning, emulated the firefighters by donning the same coats. These men became known as buffs, and, by extension, a buff is anyone avidly devoted to a pursuit or hobby.

Have you heard about the cowboy who delivered a herd of cattle to a rancher?
How many head have you got there?" asked the rancher.
"Thirty."
"Thirty? I count twenty seven."
"I rounded them up."
And have you heard about the man who gave his male offspring a cattle ranch and named it *Focus?* It was the place where the sun's rays meet—and the sons raise meat.
Is a cow who can't lactate a milk dud or an udder disaster?

To err is human, to explore cow etymologies is bovine. The cattle get your tongue till the cows come home. *Pecu* is the Latin word for cattle. Because wealth in ancient times was measured in quantity of livestock, early metal coins were stamped with the head of a bull. From this time-honored association between cattle and money we inherit the words *pecuniary,* "pertaining to money"; *impecunious,* "without money"; *peculate,* "to embezzle"; and *peculiar,* "that which is one's own."

For centuries, smallpox was a scourge of humanity, scarring, blinding, and killing millions. Edward Jenner, a British doctor, noticed that milkmaids did not generally get smallpox and theorized that the pus in the blisters that these women developed on their hands from cowpox protected them from the more virulent smallpox. In 1796, Jenner found that inoculating people with a serum containing the lymph gland fluid of cows infected with cowpox virus prevented the similar smallpox. That's why *vaccine, vaccination,* and *vaccinate* contain the Latin name for "cow," *vacca.*

The adjective *egregious* literally means "apart from the herd," from the Latin *ex-,* "out of," and *grex,* "flock." *Grex* is also the source of *gregarious,* "sociable."

When someone is *capricious* and *capers* about, they are acting like a frisky, playful goat. *Caprice, capricious, caper,* and *Capricorn* all come to us from the Latin *caper,* "goat." Goats caper through our English vocabulary.

The Italian island of Capri is so named for the goats that graze on it. A *cabriolet* was a light, two-wheeled vehicle drawn by one horse. The jaunty motion of the small carriage reminded some of the frisky leaps of a goat. *Cabriolet* ultimately shortened to *cab.*

A *goatee* is a trimmed chin beard that resembles the tufts of hair on a goat's chin. Perhaps the most famous goatee adorns the chin of our Uncle Sam.

A *scapegoat* was an actual goat upon whose head were symbolically placed all the sins of the ancient Hebrew people. As we read in the biblical Book of Leviticus, the animal was allowed to "escape" into the wilderness, bearing the community's burden of sin and atoning for its transgressions.

Goats are tragic. That is, the word *tragedy* is rooted in the Greek *tragoidia,* "goat song," because drama probably originated with the sacrifice of a scapegoat.

In U.S. slang, a goat, shortened from scapegoat, meant "a person upon whom blame is heaped for a failure." Recently, the word has gone up in the world of sports, in which *GOAT* has become an acronym for "*G*reatest *O*f *A*ll *T*ime."

Goats caper in a common American English expression. Trainers sometimes stable goats with high-strung racehorses to calm them, and the two animals can become close companions. Unscrupulous gamblers have been known to steal the goat attached to a particular horse they wanted to run poorly the next day. By extension, when we *get someone's goat*, we upset that person and throw off their performance.

Cows and goats are ruminants. When they ruminate, they bring up and chew again cud that has already been chewed and swallowed in order to digest it. By extension, when we human beings ruminate, we consider a thought or decision thoroughly.

In modern life, horses are no longer crucial in helping us to hunt, do battle, draw vehicles, or deliver mail and goods. Nevertheless, our equine friends still horse around in the figures of speech that canter—neigh, gallop—through our English language: *Healthy as a horse. Don't change horses in midstream. You can lead a horse to water, but you can't make it drink. Wild horses couldn't drag me away. I need to see a man about a horse.*

A horse is "rough-shoed" when the nails of its shoes project, ensuring a more sure-footed progress but also damaging the ground over which it gallops. Thus, when we ruthlessly advance ourselves at other people's expense, we *run roughshod* over them.

In a popular cliché, we liken a point in time to a bespurred rider mounted upon our back and urging us on with sharp prodding. Thus, we say, *on the spur of the moment*, with the rider being the moment and we being the horse. Prick up your ears and listen to how often we compare people with horses—disk jockeys, coltish lasses with ponytails, workhorses at the old stamping grounds, and dark-horse candidates.

I'm hot to trot, full of horse power, and feeling my oats—champing at the bit and eager to give unbridled free rein to talking horse sense with you about our English language. I trust that you'll maintain your equine-imity.

At the racing track, notice boards display statistics for each horse. A fan who places bets that a given horse will win, place, or show has a better chance to gain cash by betting *across the board.*

Icy balls can become packed on the hooves of horses when they are driven over soft winter snow or during spring thaws. As the footing becomes treacherous, the horses may fall, singly or in teams, producing a state of affairs that is *all balled up.*

When is a holiday not a holiday? Back in the nineteenth century, when London omnibuses (whence our word *bus*) were horse-drawn, close relationships hitched together horse teams and their drivers. The regular driver would often spend his day off riding as a passenger alongside the substitute driver in order to check his replacement's handling of the horses. That's why a vacation or day off spent doing the same thing as one's usual work is called *a busman's holiday.*

Jockeys urge their horses on by whispering "shoo" and shooing them on. Thus, a horse or a person who is an easy winner is known as a *shoo-in.*

More than five hundred years ago, the phrase *to get hitched* originated in the United States to describe tying horses to wagons. It was but a short leap for the hitching to describe two people getting married, implying that they are tied together just as a horse is tethered to a wagon.

And never forget that there are more horses' asses in the world than there are horses.

What do you get when you cross an elephant with a rhino? *Elephino.*

What do you get when you cross a sheep with a cicada? *A bah, humbug.*

The bell rings for *bellwether* because it's tied around the neck of the wether, or male sheep, that leads the flock. That's why *bellwether* usually means "a leader," but can also signify "an indicator of a trend." These days *wool gathering* means "daydreaming, aimless wandering of the mind." In days of yore, woolgathering was serious work that involved pulling tufts of sheep's wool caught on bushes or fences or left on the ground.

Thank you for allowing me to pull your eyes over the wool.

These herbivorous, hoofed creatures are but a few examples of how the critters that grace our land, sea, and air also grace our language. On-word and up-word to some other critters that grace our planet:

As descriptions of investors, *a bear market* and a *bull market* have been around since the early 1700s. The *bear market* metaphor seems to have arisen out of a story common to many cultures that tells about a man who sold a bearskin before he caught his bear. On this analogy, certain speculators in London's Exchange, the Wall Street of its day, became known as bearskin jobbers. These financial dice rollers gambled on a falling market, selling stock they didn't own in the hope that it would drop in value, before they had to deliver it to the purchaser.

The bestial analogy in *bull market* arises from how testosterone-fueled bulls push forward and toss their heads upward, an apt emblem for a market driven by investors who believe that stock prices will go up.

Biologically, a tadpole is a larval amphibian. Etymologically, *tadpole* is formed from the Middle English *tode*, "toad" + *polle*, "head," because a tadpole looks like a toad made entirely from a head, with the body and legs still to grow out. The clipped form *tad* swam into American English around 1915 with the meaning "a small amount," as in "a tad of sugar" and "a tad chilly."

I have often been asked, "In the simile *happy as a clam*, why are clams so happy?"

To arrive at an answer, one needs to know that the expression is elliptical; that is, something is left out. When we discover the missing part, we unlock the origin and true meaning of the phrase. As it turns out, the full simile is *happy as a clam at high tide*. A clam at high tide is sensibly happy because, in high water, humans can't capture the shellfish to mince, steam, bake, stuff, casino, or Rockefeller it, and high tide brings small yummy organisms to the hungry mollusk.

As for *muscle*, it is easy to see why the term derives from the Latin word *musculus*—"little mouse" because a muscle can look like something alive under our skin.

Behold the convergence of etymology and entomology. The *butterfly* may take its name from the medieval belief that these insects stole milk and butter in the dark of night. Or it may be that the creature is simply the color of butter, and it flies.

Butterfly has long befuddled language experts. It is the one common word that has no cognates—words that are similar in sound, spelling, and meaning—in related languages. What we can be sure of is that a butterfly will flutter by—and a dragonfly will drink its flagon dry.

Colors color our language—that's not just a pigment of my imagination—and the animal world gets painted by the coloring of human imagination.

Have you ever owned a white elephant? Before you shake your head no, remember that nowadays the expression *white elephant* means an object that nobody seems to want, like a huge out-of-style couch or an ugly teapot.

White elephant trumpets back to the albino elephants once considered sacred in Siam (now Thailand). These creatures were so rare that each one born became the property of the king and was not permitted to work. When a subject incurred the king's displeasure, the angry monarch would bestow as a gift one of his white elephants. The enormous appetite and utter uselessness of the animal could plunge the "gifted" man into financial ruin.

This tale and the other etymological treatises in this book are anything but red herrings. A red herring is a herring that turns red in the process of being brined and smoked. If you read English novels, you will have heard them called kippers. They're quite smelly.

There are several different proposed etymologies, but the one that seems to be most reasonable has to do with training scent hounds, for example, foxhounds. The trainer drags a red herring across the scent trail that the dog is following. The ultimate goal is to teach to dog to ignore the confusing scent and continue to follow the original trail.

Today the meaning of *red herring* has been broadened to signify "a misleading statement that diverts our attention from the real issues."

The Bird Is the Word

I'm not only a word botcher. I'm a bird watcher. So I'm going to take you under my wing and tell you that words of a feather flock together and our fowl language is strictly for the birds.

Even a bird-brained cuckoo has little trouble figuring out how we derived the noun *crane* for a hoisting machine or the verb *to crane* to depict the act of stretching one's neck to obtain a better view. But it takes an eagle eye to spot the crane hiding in *pedigree* and *cranberry*.

Perhaps you are proud of your dog's or cat's or your own pedigree, but did you know that *pedigree* gets its pedigree from the French phrase "foot of a crane" (Latin *pes*, "foot" + *de*, "of" + *grus*, "crane")? Why? Well, a little bird told me that if you trace a pedigree on a genealogical table, you find that the three-line figures of lineal descent resemble a crane's foot.

Cranberries take their name from the Low German *Kraanbere*, "crane berry," because cranes often inhabit the bogs where the berries flourish.

When exotic dancer Gypsy Rose Lee asked H. L. Mencken to coin a dignified word for a stripper, the author and critic came up with *ecdysiast*, from the Greek *ecdysis*, "to molt." The metaphoric comparison to a bird shedding its feathers is appropriate, clear, and vivid.

Believe it or not, *partridge* soars up from the Greek *perdesthai*, "to break wind," a humorous comparison to the whirring noise of the game bird's wings in flight or when flushed from cover.

Don't duck duck etymologies. The name of the fowl and the verb both derive from Old English *duce*, meaning "diver." When you duck, you stoop or bend down suddenly in the manner of a diver. We are advised to use duct tape to provide protection against hurricanes and flooding. You may be surprised to find that the original name of the cloth-backed, waterproof adhesive product was *duck tape*, so called because it repels water.

Before the adoption of the Twentieth Amendment in 1930, a president or congressman who was defeated or failed to run for re-election in November remained in office until the following March 4 (March forth!). The nickname for such hangers-on was *lame duck*, which come from an old hunter's maxim: "Never waste powder on a dead duck." Because these ducks were not entirely dead until March, some metaphor-struck jokester called them lame ducks, and the label stuck.

My purpose here is not to ruffle your feathers or get your hackles up. A hackle is a long, narrow, shiny feather on the necks of certain birds, gamecocks among them. In the heat of battle, a fighting cock's hackles become erect as a demonstration of its fury. That's why, when the going gets tough, people *get their hackles up*.

A raven has seventeen rigid feathers called pinions, while a crow has only sixteen. So the difference between a raven and a crow is just a matter of a pinion.

Chickens are the only animals you eat before they are born and after they are dead.

What kind of luggage do vultures take onto airplanes? *Carrion*.

Before the invention of the crowbar, crows had to drink at home.

You know that a bunch of sheep crowded together is a flock, a group of antelope loping together a herd, a cluster of fish swimming together a school, and a crowd of bees buzzing together a swarm.

The Bird Is the Word

But have you ever heard of a crash of rhinoceroses, a clowder of cats, a kindle of kittens, a gam of whales, or a knot of frogs?

Most of these collective nouns evolved during the Middle Ages, when the sophisticated art of hunting demanded an equally sophisticated vocabulary to name the objects of the chase. Ever since God commanded Adam to name all the creatures that run and fly and swim and crawl and burrow above, on, and under the earth, we humans have been relentless in gathering those beasts and birds into clusters.

Here's a flight of thirty avian assemblages, a groupie list that's truly for the birds:

a cast of hawks, a charm of finches, a chain of bobolinks, a congregation of plovers, a convocation of eagles

a covey of quail, a descent of woodpeckers, an exaltation of larks, a flush of mallards, a gaggle of geese

a huddle of penguins, a murder of crows (but only if there are probable caws), a murmuration of starlings, a muster of storks, a nye of pheasants,

an ostentation of peacocks, a paddling of ducks, a pandemonium of parrots, a piteousness of doves, a plump of wildfowl,

a pouch of pelicans, a rafter of turkeys, a scold of jays, a siege of herons, a tiding of magpies

a ubiquity of sparrows, an unkindness of ravens, a wake of buzzards, a watch of nightingales, a wedge of swans (when flying in a *V* formation).

A group of owls is called a parliament because an owl was often depicted accompanying Athena, the Greek goddess of wisdom. Then there's the wonderful *a flamboyance of flamingos*. Both *flamingo* and *flamboyance* descend from words referring to fire, the Spanish and Portuguese *flamengo*, "flame-colored."

Take a gander at the aviary below to come up with appropriate words and expressions to match the definitions that follow.

Sometimes the name of a given bird can stand by itself; sometimes you will have to provide a suffix or a phrase that includes a given bird, as in "low pay: *chickenfeed*." Don't quail at this challenge. Feather your nest with all the correct answers you can, and you'll really have something to crow about.

Match these bird words with the definitions that follow:

albatross	bird	buzzard	canary	catbird
chicken	cock	coot	crane	crow
cuckoo	dodo	dove	duck	eagle
gander	goose	grouse	gull	hawk
hen	lark	loon	owl	parrot
pigeon	quail	swan	turkey	vulture

1. supporter of war 2. opponent of war 3. a coward 4. the wrong direction 5. a great burden

6. a parasitical person 7. a stupid person 8. a crazy person 9. a crazy person 10. an old person

11. an old person 12. dominated by one's wife 13. a politician nearing end of term 14. one who stays up late 15. a position of advantage

16. aggressively confident 17. what humbled people eat 18. one who rats on others 19. one who rats on others 20. an escapade

21. look at 22. easily duped or cheated 23. having sharp sight 24. complain 25. suddenly, independently

26. to repeat another's words 27. one under par on a hole in golf 28. an item of heavy machinery 29. to cower 30. a farewell appearance

Answers

1. hawk 2. dove 3. chicken 4. wild goose chase 5. albatross
6. vulture 7. dodo 8. cuckoo 9. loon 10. buzzard

11. coot / crow 12. henpecked 13. lame duck 14. night owl 15. in the catbird seat

16. cocky or cocksure 17. crow 18. canary 19. stool pigeon 20. lark

21. take a gander at 22. gullible 23. eagle-eyed 24. grouse 25. cold turkey

26. parrot 27. birdie 28. crane 29. quail 30. swan song

☺Lions and Tigers and Bears

Many children's magazines feature picture puzzles that invite young readers to identify a number of hidden animals. In a cloud may lurk a cow, in the leaves of a tree may be concealed a fish, and on the side of a house may be soaring an eagle. The English language is like those children's pictures. In the following narrative, you will discover almost three hundred denizens of the animal world hidden in the sentences, a veritable class menagerie of zoological metaphors.

Human beings, proclaims one dictionary, are distinguished from the other animals "by a notable development of brain with a resultant capacity for speech and abstract reasoning." Perhaps so, but how truly different is our species from our fellow creatures who ride the planet with us?

I mean holy cow, holy cats, and holy mackerel—the human race is filled with congressional hawks and doves who fight like cats and dogs till the cows come home; Wall Street bulls and bears who make a beeline for the goose that lays the golden egg; cold fish and hotdoggers; early birds and night owls; lone wolves and social butterflies; young lions and old crows; and lucky ducks, lame ducks, sitting ducks, and dead ducks.

Some men are horny studs on the prowl for other party animals, strutting peacocks who preen and fish for compliments, and clotheshorses who put on the dog with their turtlenecks and Hush Puppies. Young bucks and ponytailed foxy chicks in puppy love and cool cats and kittenish lovebirds avoid stag parties to bill and coo and pet and paw each other in their love nests.

Lions And Tigers And Bears

Other people have a whale of an appetite. They eat like pigs (not birds), drink like fish, stuff themselves to the gills, hog the lion's share, and wolf down their elephantine portions until they become plump as partridges.

Still others are batty, squirrelly, bug-eyed, cockeyed cuckoos, who are mad as March hares and look like something the cat dragged in; crazy as coots, loons, or bedbugs who come at us like bats out of hell with their monkeyshines and drive us buggy with their horsing around.

As we continue to separate the sheep from the goats and to pigeonhole the human race, we encounter catnapping, slothful sluggards; harebrained jackasses who, like fish out of water, doggedly think at a snail's pace; dumb bunnies and dumb clucks who run around like chickens with their heads cut off; birdbrained dodos who are easily gulled, buffaloed, and outfoxed; asinine silly geese who lay an egg whenever, like monkey-see-monkey-do, they parrot and ape every turkey they see; clumsy oxen who are bulls in china shops; top dogs and rich bitches on their high horses; big fish in small ponds; and cocky bullies high up in the pecking order who rule the roost but work for chicken feed.

Leapin' lizards, we can scarcely get through a day without meeting pussyfooting chickens; henpecked underdogs who get goose bumps and butterflies and turn tail; fraidy cats who play possum and cry crocodile tears before they go belly up; spineless jellyfish who clam up with a frog in their throat whenever the cat gets their tongue; mousy worms who quail and flounder and then return to the fold with their tails between their legs; and shrimpy pipsqueaks who fawn like toadies until you want to croak.

Without beating a dead horse, I don't wish to duck under or leapfrog over this subject and go down a rabbit hole. It's time to fish or cut bait, to take the bull by the horns, kill two birds with one stone, and, before everything goes to the dogs and we've got a tiger by the tail, to give you a bird's-eye view of the animals hiding in our language.

Dog my cats! It's a bear of a task to avoid meeting catty, shrewish vixens with bees in their bonnets whose pet peeve and sacred cow is that all men are swine and chauvinist pigs who should be in the doghouse. Other brutes who get your goat and ruffle your feathers are antsy, backbiting, crabby, pigheaded old buzzards, coots, and goats who are no spring chickens, who are stubborn as mules, and who grouse, bug, badger, dog, and hound you like squawking, droning, waspish gadflies that stir up a hornets' nest and make a mountain out of a molehill.

Speaking of beastly characters that stick in your craw, watch out for

- the parasites, bloodsuckers, sponges, and leeches who worm their way into your consciousness make you their scapegoats, and turn out to be wolves in sheep's clothing
- the rat finks, weasels, canaries, and stool pigeons who ferret out your deepest secrets and then squeal on you, let the cat out of the bag, and fly the coop without so much as a "Tough turkey"
- the snakes-in-the-grass who come out of the woodwork and, before you smell a rat, open a can of worms
- the serpentine quacks who make you their gullible guinea pig and cat's-paw with all their hogwash before they hightail it out of there
- the lowdown curs and dirty dogs who sling the bull and send you on a wild goose chase barking up the wrong tree
- the card sharks who hawk their fishy games, monkey with your nest egg, put the sting on you, sell you a white elephant, and then fleece you
- the vultures who hang like albatrosses around your neck, who live high on the hog, who feather their own nests, and then—the straw that breaks the camel's back—crow about it, looking like the cat that swallowed the canary

- the black sheep who play cat and mouse and then cook your goose, make a monkey out of you with their shaggy dog stories
- and the lousy varmints, polecats, and skunks, who sell you a pig in a poke and, when the worm turns and you discover the fly in the ointment, weasel their way out of the deal.

But let's talk turkey. Don't we go ape and hog wild over the bright-eyed and bushy-tailed eager beavers who are always loaded for bear, go whole hog to hit the bull's-eye, and have all their ducks in a row and the ducky rare birds who are wise as owls and happy as larks and clams? Lucky dogs like these are the cat's pajamas and the cat's meow, worthy of being lionized. From the time they're knee-high to a grasshopper, they're in the catbird seat, and the world is their oyster. We get goose bumps just thinking about them.

So before you buzz off, I hope you'll agree that this exhibit of animal metaphors has been no fluke and no hogwash. I really give a hoot about the animals hiding in our English language, so for my swan song, I want you to know that, straight from the horse's mouth, this has been no dog-and-pony show or cock-and-bull story.

Life is a jungle, just one unbridled rat race, and the rats are winning. It really is a zoo out there.

THE CAT'S GOT OUR TONGUE

The poet Carl Sandburg wrote, "The fog comes in on little cat feet." So does a prodigious litter of our words and expressions. Whatever their ups and downs throughout history, cats have usually landed on their feet and have left their paw prints on our mother tongue.

Let's categorize the cats that run and leap and pounce and slink and purr and meow through our English language. I hope you'll find them to be, in the idiom of the roaring twenties, *the cat's meow, the cat's pajamas,* and *the cat's whiskers,* so called because the cat is capable of looking enormously pleased and satisfied.

Quick as a cat, let's make a "feline" for cat words in our English language:

The words *cat* and *pussy* derive from the Latin and Anglo Saxon names for the animal—*cattus* and *puus. Cattus* cocoons in the word *caterpillar,* a coalescence of the Latin elements *cattus* + *pilosus* – "hairy cat."

In some African languages, a man is referred to as a cat, which in American slang gives us the likes of *cool cat, hepcat,* and *fat cat.*

Cats bring forth kittens, and so does our English language. *Kitty-cornered* issues from "cater-cornered," which comes from "quatre-cornered," which in French originally meant "four-cornered." By a process called folk etymology, speakers thought that in "quatre – cornered" they were hearing an analogy to a certain domestic feline. In the card game of faro the tiger was the bank or house, possibly because the tiger was once used on signs marking the entrance to Chinese gambling houses. Over the years, gamblers transformed the tiger into a *kitty*, and it became the name for the pot in poker and other card games. Thus, when one contributes to the common store of betting money, one *sweetens* (or fattens) *the kitty.*

Let's do some cat-and-mouse phrase origins. Have you heard about the cat that ate some strong-smelling cheese, breathed into a mouse hole, and waited with baited breath? That joke plays on the same sound of *baited* and *bated,* a clipping of *abated,* which means "hold back, diminish."

When the pussycat is absent (or taking a *catnap*), the mice have free run of the place, and *when the cat's away, the mice will play,* a proverb that reposes in many languages.

Cats, of course, have long been belled to prevent them from killing songbirds, but the expression *to bell the cat,* meaning "to take on a dangerous mission at great personal risk for the benefit of others," derives from the observation of a wise mouse. In one of Aesop's fables, the mice held a general council to consider what measures they could take to outwit their common enemy, the Cat. A young mouse stood up and said: "I propose that a small bell be procured, and attached by a ribbon around the neck of the Cat. By this means we should always know when the Cat is in the neighborhood." The proposal was met with general applause, until an old mouse rose and said, "That's all very well, but who will bell the cat?" The mice looked around at one another, and nobody spoke.

In the arena of cat-and-mouse etymology, we find a curious relationship between social history and phrase origins. Surprisingly, feminists arrested during the suffragette agitation in England in about 1913 inspired the first popular use of the expression *to play cat and mouse with.* When imprisoned, the suffragettes often went on hunger strikes, and the British Parliament retaliated by passing the Prisoners' Temporary Discharge for Ill-Health Act. The bill provided that hunger strikers be set free while fasting, but, when they recovered, they were liable for rearrest to complete their sentences.

Critics compared the government's action to a big cat playing with a little mouse and dubbed the legislation "The Cat and Mouse Act," which entered common parlance as *to play cat and mouse with*.

Harking back to their larger and fiercer ancestors, many cats have a passion for chipmunks, field mice, birds, and other outdoor animals. They proudly deposit the corpses at their owners' doorsteps or behind and under furniture, a practice that gave rise, about 1920, to the expression *looking like something the cat dragged in*. While cats are valued for hunting pests, they do not always discriminate among their prey, and the cat that goes after its owner's prized pet bird may be in for a good scolding. *To look like the cat that ate the canary* originally meant to look guilty, but nowadays means to appear smug and self-satisfied.

Why can't some animals keep secrets? Because pigs squeal, yaks yak, and someone always lets the cat out of the bag. Not long ago, city slickers had to beware of buying a pig in a poke (bag) from a farmer who wasn't in any way a country bumpkin. The animals inside such pokes were sometimes cats or kittens the canny country folk had substituted for suckling pigs. When the merchant opened the poke, he often *let the cat out of the bag,* revealing the crafty farmer's secret. When the cat ran off, the city bumpkin was left *holding the bag.*

When a cat is attacked by a dog or other animal, it aggressively arches its back, a response that suggested the phrase *to get one's back up* to describe humans aroused into anger. On the other paw, cats are often pictured as grinning. Charles Lutwidge Dodgson, best known to the world as Lewis Carroll, popularized the Cheshire Cat in his children-of-all-ages classic, *Alice's Adventures in Wonderland* (1865). The Cheshire Cat in the story gradually faded from Alice's view, its smile being the last part of the animal to vanish. *To grin like a Cheshire Cat* reaches back before Carroll, and the source could be Cheshire cheeses, which were at one time molded in the form of a cat. Another theory contends that the cat grins because the former palatine of Cheshire once had regal privileges in England, paying no taxes to the crown.

The phrase *having kittens* suggests a condition of severe anxiety. In bygone, more superstitious days, pregnant women who experienced long, painful labors were thought to be bewitched and about to give birth to a litter of felines.

An old British expression advised that "There's more than one way of killing a cat than choking it with cream." This implied that a method of doing something was rather foolish, since cats like cream and wouldn't be able to choke to death on it. But the saying changed to *There's more than one way to skin a cat* and gradually took on its present meaning—that there are more ways than one of accomplishing something.

Both the droopy *pussy willow* and the tall, reedlike *cattail* are so called for their resemblance to a cat's freely swinging tail. Because of that visual similarity and because it "scratched" the back like a cat, some black humorist coined the name *cat-o'-nine-tails* for the terrible whip. In addition, the first Egyptian scourges were made of thongs of cat hide.

Cats have long been regarded as tenacious of life because of their careful, suspicious nature and because they are supple animals that can survive long falls. The old English saying *a cat has nine lives* goes back well before the sixteenth century, and the nine "tails" of the whip being similar to the nine lives of a cat might have suggested the full name *cat-o'-nine tails*.

When we say or write *no room to swing a cat*, we are not referring to the animal but to the knotted cat-o'-nine-tails whip used to punish disobedient sailors. The scourge was too long to swing below deck, so punishment was always applied outdoors and left scars like those from a cat's scratch.

This shortening of the name of the whip to *cat* also explains the title of this chapter. The anticipation of a beating by the cruel cat-o'-nine-tails could paralyze a victim into silence. That's why *Has the cat got your tongue?* came to mean "Are you unable to speak?"

The Dog's Got Our Tongue

Why do we love thee, doggies? Let us count the ways. Dogs are highly companionable, obedient, and playful animals. No other creature on earth shares our homes and our lives the way dogs do. The partnership is unique in interspecies relationships. The loyalty and devotion that dogs demonstrate as part of their natural pack-animal instincts exemplifies the human idea of love and friendship. Dogs seem to view their humans as members of their pack, and the same goes for most dog owners. To us, dogs are adopted sons and daughters who are short, hairy, walk on all fours, and possess rudimentary speech. Like cats, dogs leave their paw prints on our hearts and our language.

How do you know when it's raining cats and dogs? *When you step in a poodle!*

Bwa-ha-ha! So funny—but the riddle is etymologically spot on. The word *poodle*, which designates a curly-haired water dog, started life as *Pudelhund,* German for "splash" + "dog."

Ah, the joy of etymology!

The word *dog* trots, prances, scampers, races, and barks through our marvelous English language. We call a tenacious person a bulldog, a showoff a hot dog, a fortunate person a lucky dog, a man with an active social life a gay dog who puts on the dog ("makes a flashy display"), and a rapscallion a cur or dirty dog. A dominant person is a top dog who can run with the big dogs, while his counterpart is an underdog. Some of us lead a dog's life going to the dogs in the doghouse. Others are young pups in puppy love.

It's sad how dogs, those most loyal and loving of creatures, are treated so shabbily in our English language. It's distressingly easy to think of common words and expressions that are negative about dogs—*bitch, cur, hangdog, underdog, dog tired, a dog's life, dog days, you dirty dog, sick as a dog, in the doghouse, you're dogging it, going to the dogs, hot dogger, you're dog meat, you can't teach an old dog new tricks, his bark is worse than his bite*—on and on it goes. But why don't we say *cute as a dog, amiable as a dog, loyal as a dog, loving as a dog*? How many positive canine words and phrases leap to your mind? Not many.

One of the most endearing characteristics of dogs is fidelity to their owners, which has made dogs valued companions. As long ago as 1150, the learned St. Bernard of Clairvaux said, *"Qui me amat, amat et canem meam."* That translates to "Love me, love my dog"—an expression of unconditional affection that reposes in many languages. That's a *dog-eared* phrase, so called because a page in a well-worn book can get folded over like the ear of a dog.

Other canine proverbs yip and bark across centuries. In Geoffrey Chaucer's fourteenth century tale of *Troilus and Creseyde*, the poet writes, "It is nought good a sleping hound to wake," which comes down to us as *Let sleeping dogs lie*.

Another expression derived from literature is *in the doghouse*, which means "out of favor with the powers that be." The first appearance of this phrase occurs in James Barrie's play *Peter Pan* (1904). Mr. Darling, the father of the three children, is punished for his shabby treatment of Nana, the Newfoundland dog, who is also the children's nurse. And where does Mr. Darling spend his exile? In Nana's doghouse, of course.

Sometimes dogs fight with other dogs over a single bone, a scene that gives us the phrase *bone of contention*. This transfer of a canine dog fight to a human quarrel began as a *bone of dissension:* "This became a bone of dissension between these deere friends," – William Lambarde, 1576.

A *three-dog night* is not only a popular music group of the 1970s, but a night so cold that one must sleep with three dogs in order to generate enough body heat to be comfortable.

Dog eat dog dates from the sixteenth century, even though Marcus Teretius Varro in 43 B.C. reminded us that *"Canis caninam non est"*—"Dogs are not cannibals." Even more ancient is the proverbial "dog in a manger," from an Aesop's fable written around 570 B.C. about a snarling dog who prevents oxen from eating their corn, even though the dog himself doesn't want it.

In the early nineteenth century in American English, *barker* came to signify the person who stands outside a carnival or circus to shout (bark) out its attractions to passersby. From the same period in the United States arose the expression *to bark up the wrong tree,* from hunting dogs that mistakenly crowd around the base of a tree thinking they have treed a raccoon that has actually taken a different route. The phrase is still used to mean wasting one's energy by pursuing the wrong path.

Another classic Americanism is *hot dog*. In nineteenth-century America, some folks suspected that sausages were made from dog meat, as evidenced by this popular ditty:

> Oh where, oh where has my little dog gone?
> Oh where, oh where can he be?
> Now sausage is good, baloney, of course.
> Oh where, oh where can he be?
> They make them of dog, they make them of horse.
> I think they made them of he.

When hot sausages in a bun became popular, it was but a short leap to the term *hot dog*. Cartoonist Tad Dorgan featured the hot dog in some of his sports cartoons, helping to popularize the new name. That the sausage looks a little like the body of a Dachshund also helped the *hot dog* to cleave to the American palate.

The dachshund is one of the oldest dog breeds in history, dating back to ancient Egypt. The name and the low, sleek body reflect one of its earliest uses—flushing badgers and other underground animals from their holes. In German, *Dachs* means "badger" and *Hund* means "hound." When people buy a Dachshund, they sing, "Get a Long Little Doggie."

The most misspelled dog breed is the name for those handsome canines with the short white coat and the dappling of black spots. No, I'm not talking about *Dalmations*. I'm talking about *Dalmatians*, so spelled because the breed is said to have originated in Dalmatia, a peninsula on the Adriatic Sea.

We could talk about dogs in our language until the last dog is hung. Here the reference is to the dirty dog of the human species who rustled your cattle, and the *hung is* to the vigilante lynchings known as "necktie parties" in the early West. Nowadays the expression most often points to the inevitable two or three people at every party who hang around everlastingly—until the last dog is hung and the host shows them to the door.

What's in a Name?

Never pride yourself on your knowledge. Always remember that a little knowledge is a dangerous thing—especially when you discover that Alexander Pope actually wrote that famous quotation as "A little *learning* is a dangerous thing."

Here's a test of your knowledge of the animal kingdom. The Canary Islands in the Atlantic got their name from what creature?

"Canaries, of course!" you chirp.

Wrong.

The answer is large dogs, i.e. canines. The Latin name was *Canaria insulae*, "Dogs Islands." Canaries got their name from the islands, not the other way around.

How many legs does a centipede have? Judging by the name (Latin: "hundred feet"), you probably reply, "a hundred."

Wrong again.

The number of legs on a centipede varies from thirty to 354. Each segment has a pair of legs, but the number of segments is always odd. Hence, no centipede has exactly a hundred legs. Similarly, no millipede (Latin: "thousand feet") is equipped with more than 750 feet.

We have named a super-intelligent mollusk *octopus*, from the Greek *oktō*, "eight" + *pous*, "foot." So how many legs does an octopus have?

Despite the etymology, the answer is two. The other six are arms.

In our ginormous but erratic English vocabulary, we discover that catgut is usually sheep, goat, cattle, hog, horse, mule, or donkey intestines and that camel hair brushes are made from squirrel fur.

A ladybug is a beetle, and they're not all females. A lightning bug is also a beetle. And a firefly is actually a lightning bug, which, as you now know, is a beetle. Wormwood is a European plant that yields a bitter-tasting oil but contains neither worm nor wood.

In fact, a whole menagerie of animals are not what their names indicate. Take the hedgehog. Light verse master Bob McKenty explains the truth about the spiny insectivore:

No matter what their name alleges,
Hedgehogs aren't hogs or hedges
(Like kindred quadrupeds with spines
Who aren't porks and aren't pines).

The blackbird hen is brown, purple finches are distinctly raspberry red, and many greyhounds come in colors other than gray. The *grey* hails from an Old Icelandic root that means "bitch," and, of course, half of all greyhounds aren't bitches.

The koala bear is a marsupial, not a bear. The guinea pig is a South American rodent. It is neither a pig nor from Guinea. A prairie dog is not a dog; it too is a rodent. The horned toad is a lizard, not a toad, while a silkworm is not a worm; it's a caterpillar. The killer whale is not a whale; it's a dolphin. Half of peacocks are actually peahens. A titmouse is neither mammaried nor mammal; it's a bird. Crawfish, starfish, cuttlefish, and jellyfish are not actually fish. The only thing they have in common with fish is their habitat. Silverfish also aren't fish. They're insects. Electric eels aren't eels: They are closer to carp and catfish. A jackrabbit is a hare, not a rabbit. A bald eagle isn't bald. Its head is adorned with white feathers. Blindworms are actually legless lizards, and, of course, they can see.

😀Animal Advice

Here's hoping that this collection of beastly puns may help you succeed in a dog-eat-dog world in which the fittest survive:

- Be like a turtle. You'll make progress by coming out of your shell and sticking your neck out.
- Speaking of sticking your neck out, be like a giraffe. Reach higher than all the others, and you'll have the best perspective on life. Stand tall, and the general herd will look up to you.
- Be like the birds. They have bills, too, but they keep on singing.
- Be like a duck. Keep calm and unruffled on the surface, but paddle like crazy underneath.
- Be like a beaver. Don't get stumped. Just cut things down to size and build one dammed thing after another.
- Be like a cat. Claw your way to the top. That's what drapes are for.
- Be like a big cat. Have a roaring good time, live life with pride, and grab the lion's share with might and mane.
- Be like a dog. Be loyal. Enjoy the wind in your face. Run barefoot, romp, and play daily. Leave yourself breathless at least once a day. Don't chase your tail in an effort to make ends meet. And be sure to leave your mark on the world.
- Be like a chicken. Act like a smart cluck and rule the roost. Be proud when you lay an egg.

Animal Advice

- Be like a horse. Use some horse sense and stable thinking and be able to say, "neigh."
- Be like an owl. Look all around, be wise, and give a hoot.
- Be like a rhino. Be thick-skinned and charge ahead to make your point.
- Be like an oyster. It takes grit to make a pearl of great value.
- Be like a sponge. Soak up everything and be helpful in the kitchen.
- Be like a spider. Pull the right strings and surf the web.
- Be like a squirrel. Go out on a limb to prepare for hard times.
- Be like a kangaroo. Advance through life by leaps and bounds, and keep your family close to you.
- Be like a frog. Be comfortable on land and water—and if something bugs you, snap it up.
- Be like a mole. Stay down-to-earth and well-grounded. Forge ahead by digging as deep as you can.
- Be like a flamingo. Don't be afraid of looking odd, as long as you have a leg to stand on.
- Be like a peacock. Show off your true colors, and strut your stuff.
- Be like a caterpillar. Eat a lot, sleep for a while, and wake up beautiful.
- Be like the woodpecker. Just keep pecking away until you finish the job. You'll succeed by using your head and proving that opportunity knocks more than once.
- Don't be like a lemming. Avoid following the crowd and jumping to conclusions.
- And remember that the only things you find in the middle of the road are yellow stripes and dead armadillos.

As your reader-friendly Attila the pun, my final Gnu Year's resolution is to tell ewe a gazelleon times how much I caribou ewe, deer. I'm a wildebeest of a punster, and you're thinking, "Unicorniest fellow I've ever met!" But I'm not out to buffalo or a llama ewe, so alpaca bag and hightail it out of here in camelflage.

Land, Sea, Air, and Beyond

Down-to-Earth Metaphors

We were once a nation of farmers, but by the turn of the twentieth century, most had moved to towns and cities. Today only two percent of Americans live on farms, and many have lost touch with our agricultural roots. In "God's Grandeur" (1877), the Jesuit poet Gerard Manley Hopkins lamented how the Industrial Age has ravaged our feeling for the land:

> And all is seared with trade;
> bleared, smeared with toil;
> And wears man's smudge
> and shares man's smell: the soil
> Is bare now, nor can foot feel, being shod.

Even though our shod feet may no longer touch the soil, most Americans speak and write the metaphors that spring from the earth and those who work it. These verbal seeds lie buried so deeply in the humus of our language that we are hardly aware that they are figures of speech at all. Let's do some digging to uncover the rich, earthy agriculture from which grow so much of our speech and our writing, our thoughts and our dreaming.

Our fertile English language is cultivated by agricultural comparisons, and they're not like trying to find a needle in a haystack. Why can't you keep a secret in a field of crops? *Because the corn has ears, the potatoes have eyes, and the beanstalk.*

Down-to-earth metaphors cut a wide swath: *a vintage year, a grass roots campaign, a budding movie star, gone to seed, seed money, seedy, cut and dried, farm team, reap the benefits, mow down, separate the wheat from the chaff, cut a wide swath, crop up, feel one's oats, farm out, weed out, plow into,* and *the grass is always greener on the other side.*

The song lyrics "This land is your land, and this land is my land" are so very true. Here, unearthed, is a bountiful crop of agricultural words and phrases:

Among the down-to-earth figures of speech that are planted in our language is the word *broadcast,* which first meant "to broadly cast seed on the ground by hand" and in 1922 took on its modern meaning with the emergence of radio.

The lines in a worried forehead resemble the grooves in the earth made by a plow. We describe such a forehead as *furrowed.*

Like well-farmed land, the fertile minds of those who read this book are carefully tended and yield a bountiful harvest. We say that such people are *cultivated.*

A harrow is a cultivating farm implement set with spikes or spring teeth that pulverize the earth by violently tearing and flipping over the topsoil. That's why we identify an emotionally lacerating experience as *harrowing.*

A mentally talented child is often identified as *precocious,* from the Latin *praecox,* "ripe before its time."

European peasants, forbidden to cut down or pick from trees, were allowed to gather wood and fruit blown down by the wind, a bounty that required little effort on the part of the lucky recipients. By extension, we today use a word that describes an unexpected stroke of good luck: *a windfall.*

Rooted in the Latin *de-,* "from," and *lira,* "furrow," is a word that metaphorically compares behavior that deviates from a straight course and swerves from the conventional path in plowing: *delirious.*

In bygone days, the Old English *math* meant "mowing." Nowadays a word that means "results, effects, or consequences" is an *aftermath.*

The arduous job of hoeing long rows in uncooperative terrain gives us *a hard* (or *tough*) *row to hoe,* an expression that means "a difficult task."

Down-to-Earth Metaphors

Late spring frosts or pests can kill an aborning leaf or flower before it has a chance to develop. When we terminate a project in its early stages, we say that we *nip it in the bud.*

Hay is made by setting mown grass out in the sun to dry. When we want to make the most of an opportunity, we *make hay while the sun shines.*

Anyone who has ever tried to cut the tightly stretched baling wire used to bind a bale of hay knows how ornery the stuff can be. When someone or something behaves in an uncontrolled manner, we say that he, she, or it goes *haywire.*

In the word *towhead, tow* descends from an Old English word that means "flax." A towhead is a youngster—usually male, but not necessarily so—with white or pale yellow hair the color of flax. Avoid confusing *tow* with *toe,* as in this newspaper photo caption: "Linda Tinyon clutched her toe-headed son during the storm." Even worse: "Linda Tinyon clutched her two-headed son during the storm."

A popular toast rings out, *Here's mud in your eye,* which originally meant "May you find soft, rich, dark, and moist soil that will be thrown up as specks of mud as you plow it."

Much newer than these agricultural metaphors is *couch potato,* which made its debut in U.S. slang in the 1970s. The compound compares lumpish watchers of television to lumpy potatoes: The longer couch potatoes sit, the deeper they put down their roots and the more they come to resemble potatoes. But there's more than just a vegetable image here. In *The Real McCoy,* George Hole explains: "The origins of the phrase are much cleverer than simply an image, however, since it actually relies on a pun with the word *tuber.* A potato is the tuber of a plant, while *boob tuber* was an earlier term for someone watching the *boob tube* or television."

Shaped from the pattern *of couch potato,* we now have *mouse potato, mouse* referring to the electronic mouse that helps you navigate your computer. A *mouse potato* is someone who lives a sedentary life, spending great gobs of leisure time playing computer games, surfing the net, streaming videos, and falling headlong into the screen.

An Anthology of Flowery Words

An anthology is a collection of literary, musical or artistic works gathered in a single setting. The Greek forebear is *anthologia*: *anthos*, "flower" + *lego*, "gather" = "a gathering of flowers." Just as our land is beautified by a vast array of flowers dappling its hills, fields, gardens, and median strips, our English language is made more exquisite and colorful by an anthology of flowery words:

Because the bright yellow *cowslip* thrives in pasturelands, it shares a name with something else found in pastures—cow dung.

In Greek mythology, the blessed spent their afterlife in the Elysian fields, which were carpeted with a flower the Greeks named *asphodelos*. Over time the word gained an initial *d* and eventually became *daffodil*. LID OFF A DAFFODIL is a palindrome, a phrase that reads the same forward and backward.

Daisy was created in Old English from the poetical "day's eye." The flower is indeed a metaphor waiting to be born, with its sunburst center, its radiating white petals, and its sensitivity to the progress of the day, opening during the sunny hours and closing in the evening and extinguishing its brightness. The poet Geoffrey Chaucer, without benefit of any linguistic manual, referred to the sun as "the day's eye, or else the eye of day." On a more macabre note, the daisy is also the focus in the slangy *pushing up the daisies*, an informal way of saying "dead and buried."

Many members of the *geranium* family exhibit long, thin, tapering fruits that resemble the beak of a bird. That's why the Greeks named the flower *geranion*, "little crane."

Iris was originally the Greek word for both "rainbow" and for the goddess of rainbows. who left a trail of color as she delivered messages. Later her name was applied to the colorful flower and to the thin, circular structure in our eyes that gives them color.

The *orchid* is not named for its elegant blossoms but for its twin bulbs, which, in the eyes of many, resemble male gonads. That's why the name of the beautiful and expensive flower is rooted in the Greek word for "testicle," *orkhis*, which literally means "testicle." More than two thousand years ago, Pliny the Elder observed, "*Mirabilis est orkhis herba, sive serapias, gemina radice, testiculis simili.*" Even if you don't know Latin, I'm confident that you can deduce the meaning of the first and last parts of that statement. Pliny believed that just holding an orchid in one's hand would heighten sexual desire.

The *passionflower* was so christened not because it inspired romantic love but because parts of the flowery vine resemble the cross on which the Passion of Christ took place.

The *rose* holds a special significance in our bouquet of flowery language, which is abundant with rose idioms that often seem to be inspired by the flower's pleasant scent and beauty. *Take time to smell the roses* is to appreciate what is often ignored. If you come out *smelling like a rose*, you have emerged from a difficult situation with your reputation intact. A similar optimism perfumes *a bed of roses, everything's coming up roses, rose-colored glasses,* and *a rosy outlook*. Then there's Gertrude Stein's epiphanous "Rose is a rose is a rose."

The *tulip*'s large, cup-shaped "mouth" may remind you of "two lips," but that's not how the blossom got its name. The Dutch borrowed *tulip* from the French (*tulipan*), who purloined it from the Turks, who noted that the shape of the flower reminded them of a turban.

A garden of women's first names bloom from flowers—Acacia, Amaryllis, Blossom, Buttercup, Camellia, Cherry, Dahlia, Daisy,

Danica, Flora, Gardenia, Hazel, Heather, Holly, Hyacinth, Iris, Ivy, Jasmine, Laurel, Leilani, Lily, Lotus, Magnolia, Marguerite, Marigold, Myrtle, Orchid, Pansy, Peony, Petunia, Poppy, Posey, Rhoda, Rose, Rue, Shoshanna, Susannah, Veronica, Violet, Willow, Yasmin, Yolanda, and Zenobia.

While most perennials flower, they are plants, not flowers. My eighty-and-over *generation* (jocularly "a ration of genes") has been dubbed *old timers, the silent generation, senior citizens, golden agers, retirees,* and—ew!—*fuddy-duddies, duffers, old goats, geezers, coots, codgers, bags, biddies,* and *farts*. I propose the sobriquet *perennials*. As I hope this book demonstrates, we're still blooming!

Our Seaworthy Language

In "Sea Fever" (1902), the poet John Masefield penned:

> I must go down to the seas again,
> To the lonely sea and the sky,
> And all I ask is a tall ship
> And a star to steer her by.

Relatively few of us go down to the seas, and even fewer of us get to steer a tall ship. Nevertheless, we still taste the salty flavor of the nautical metaphors that ebb and flow through our language.

Consider our use of the word *ship*. We continue to ship goods, even when we ship by truck, train, or plane. We compliment someone on running a tight ship, even when that ship is an office or a classroom. And many things besides ships can be shipshape or sinking ships.

The lapping of the sea at our language is not a difficult concept to fathom. When we try to fathom an idea, we are making poetic use of an old word that originally meant "the span between two outstretched arms." Then the word came to designate "a unit of six feet used for measuring the depth of water." By poetic extension, the verb *to fathom* now means "to get to the bottom of something," and that something doesn't have to be the ocean.

To help you learn the ropes and get your bearings with stem-to-stern seafaring metaphors, take a turn at the helm. The coast is clear for you to take a different tack. Don't go overboard by barging ahead and rocking the boat. If you feel all washed up, on the rocks, in over your head, or sinking fast in a wave of confusion, try to batten down the hatches, clear the deck, and stay on an even keel. As your friendly anchorman, I won't lower the boom on you.

Now that you get my drift, consider how the following idioms of sailing and the sea wash up on the shores of our everyday vocabulary: *shape up or ship out, take the wind out of his sails, the tide has turned, we're all in the same boat, a sea of faces, down the hatch, hit the deck, steer clear of, harbor a grudge, take a different tack, cruise to victory, smooth sailing, don't make waves,* and *give a wide berth to.*

As attractive an explanation as it might be, *to deep six* had nothing to do with burying a body six feet deep or by walking the plank. It's a naval idiom that means "to throw overboard," with *six* signifying "six fathoms [thirty-six feet] deep." The original term came from measuring the water depth under a ship using a lead-weighted sounding line. The lines were marked at two, three, five, seven, ten, thirteen, fifteen, seventeen, and twenty fathoms. If the depth was at a mark, the leadsman would call "by the mark," followed by the number. If the depth was between two marks, he would call "by the deep" followed by the estimated number. Six fathoms would be "by the deep six." By extension, *to deep six* has come to denote generally "to get rid of someone or something."

As a barefoot boy sitting on the banks of the Mississippi River, Samuel Clemens watched stern-wheeler boats churning the muddy waters, and he heard the leadsmen sounding the depth of the river by calling out to the captains, "By the deep six... by the mark five... by the deep four... by the mark three." When the river bottom was only two fathoms, or twelve feet down, he would hear the lusty cry "by the mark twain." After he left the Mississippi, and after various careers as a riverboat pilot, prospector, and printer, Sam Clemens, now a journalist, contributed an article to the *Nevada Territorial Enterprise* on February 3, 1863, and signed it with a new name—Mark Twain.

For ancient mariners, *by and large* meant "in general; for the most part." It's a nautical term in two parts. *By* means "to sail into the wind" while *large* means "to sail with the wind at your back." To say that a ship sailed well by and large meant that it sailed successfully in all conditions, passing the test with flying colors. When we say *by and large* today, we still mean "in general; for the most part" because we do not wish to sail directly into the topic. A similar sounding phrase *full and by* has a different meaning. To sail full and by is to sail into the wind, keeping the sails full of all the wind possible.

The expression *taken aback* probably conjures up in your mind an image of a person caught off guard and staggering backwards. But the origin of the phrase is nautical, too. Sailing *full and by* left an inexperienced helmsman in danger of being taken aback, which meant "to catch the wind on the wrong side of the sails." That could drive the ship backward and even break the mast.

I trust you won't be taken aback by the armada of additional salty words and seafaring metaphors:

For time immemorial a *figurehead* has been a wooden statue carved on the prow of a ship and looking down at the waves. These figures were meant to placate the gods and the sea and ensure a safe voyage. Now we think of a figurehead as someone who has the appearance of high rank but in reality holds no power.

The lee is the leeward side of the ship sheltered from the wind. Leeway is the sideways drift of a ship to the leeward side, away from the wind. Hence, when we make things easy for others, we give them *leeway,* extra space.

On sailing ships of yesteryear, the *butt* was a name for a large, lidded cask that held drinking water. These butts were equipped with "scuttles," openings through which sailors ladled out the water. Just as today's office workers gather around a water cooler to exchange chitchat and rumor, crewmen stood about the scuttled butts to trade *scuttlebutt.*

The idiom that old salts used to describe a ship in shallow water that touched bottom from time to time has been extended to designate any precarious situation or narrow escape as *touch-and-go.* A much worse predicament is one in which a ship strikes bottom and is held tight, unable to proceed. Today we use the expression *hard and fast* to identify any rigid rule or opinion. Similarly, like a vessel driven ashore beyond the normal high-water mark, one who is abandoned or rejected, is *left high and dry*.

The doldrums are those parts of the ocean near the Equator that are noted for calm winds. They pose no difficulty for fuel-driven vessels, but sailing ships can be stuck dead in the water for weeks. When we are stuck in boredom or depression, we are *in the doldrums*.

For sailors, *sheets* refer to the lines (ropes) attached to the lower corners of a sail to hold it in place. If any of the sheets came loose, the sails flapped in the wind like flags, the vessel lost power, and the crew lost control. When three sheets of on old sailing vessel broke loose, the ship would lurch, stagger, and roll from side to side like a sailor inebriated. That's why we call an unsteady state of drunkenness *three sheets to the wind*.

From the Greek word for "ship," we inherit a word that means "illness" but that originally signified "seasickness." That word is *nausea*. If you've taken a cruise and spent the first day staring at the rolling water and depositing your lunch into it, you'll appreciate the bond between *nautical* and *nausea*.

Because a mainstay is a strong rope that helps stabilize a ship's main mast, but for most of us *mainstay* means "the most important part of something; someone or something that provides primary support." In the same fleet as *mainstay* sails *flagship*, a ship that carries the commander's flag and has come to mean "the best and most important of a group."

Seafaring folk call the two posts fixed to the deck for securing the anchor line the *bitt*s and a turn of rope or chain around the bitts the *bitter*. The *bitter end* refers to the final part of the anchor line near where it is fixed to the ship's bitts. When the line is paid out, sailors lowering an anchor know that only a few yards of anchor rope remain. The men have reached the end of their rope, which is just the place that this salty disquisition has reached—*the bitter end.*

To dock this nautical disquisition, I proffer one of my favorite Irish toasts:

> There are good ships, and there are wood ships,
> The ships that sail the sea,
> But the best ships are friendships.
> May they always be.

CANOE

Well, actually we're not at the end of our voyage through seafaring words and phrases. Some witty wordsmith has invented the acronym CANOE to stand for "*C*ommittee *A*scribing *N*autical *O*rigins to *E*verything." That committee boasts thousands of members.

They claim, for example, that the expression *three square meals* originated from the Royal Navy's protocol for serving food. While the officers and captain used silver and dined off china, common seamen were issued wooden spoons to eat off square wooden plates. Such plates do exist, so why not make up a plausible story that connects *square meal* with the wooden-plate artifacts? Somebody did just that, and, ever since, tour guides have perpetuated the entertaining rubbish.

Balderdash! Twaddle! Codswollop! The word *square* has many meanings, including "proper, honest, straightforward," as in *square deal* and *fair and square*; and that's the meaning in *square meal*. No record from any sailing vessel supports the wooden-plate theory, while print citations for *square meal* with the meaning "a good and satisfying spread" abound.

One of the most bogus of acronymic etymologies is the recurrent wheeze that *posh*, "elegant, swanky," is an acronym for "*p*ort *o*ut, *s*tarboard *h*ome," a beguiling bit of linguistic legerdemain that has taken in a company of estimable scholars. When British colonial emissaries and wealthy vacationers made passage to and from India and the Orient, they often traveled along the coast of Africa on the Peninsular and Oriental Steam Navigation Company line. Many of these travelers sought ideal accommodations "away from the weather," on the more comfortable or shady side of the ship. By paying for two staterooms—one portside out, the other starboard home—the very rich could avoid the blazing sun and strong winds both ways, an act of conspicuous consumption that has become synonymous with anything luxurious and ultrasmart.

While the abundant inventiveness here deserves at least a sitting ovation, this etymology of *posh* is, well, bosh. For one thing, neither the travelers' literature of the period nor the records of the Peninsular and Oriental Steam Navigation Company show a jot of reference to *posh*. For another thing, *posh* does not show up in print until 1918.

The editors of the *Oxford English Dictionary* say nothing of any connection with the location of cabins on ships and either ignore or reject outright the acronymic theory, and the Merriam-Webster dictionaries list the origin as "unknown." More likely and more mundanely, *posh* hails from a British slang word of the same spelling that means "a dandy."

Other exhibits of CANOE, such as *between the devil and the deep blue sea* and *under the weather,* simply don't hold water and are up the creek without a paddle. In these instances non-nautical meanings are attested to long before these phrases appeared in any nautical sense, and ship's logs are devoid of the bogus seafaring definitions. Caring and careful linguists try to avoid foisting such "internetymology" on their readers, which is why I didn't infect the previous chapter with such linguistic blarney.

Under the Weather

You probably think about the weather almost every day, but have you ever noticed how much our speech is affected by weather words? Some people strike us as chilly, cool, cold, icy, or frigid, while others seem to radiate a warm and sunny disposition. Because temperature, moisture, and wind conditions are so important in our lives, a variety of weather patterns blow hot and cold through many of the descriptive phrases in our speech and writing.

The word *hurricane* blows in from the Arawakan (West Indies) name for the Caribbean god Juracán, "evil spirit of the sea." In 1953 the National Weather Service began conferring female first names on all hurricanes, categorizing those devastating winds as female. When I was a boy, we bandied about a little riddle: "Why do they give hurricanes female names?" "Because otherwise, they'd be himicanes!" Har, har! Chuckle, chuckle! Snort!

That riddle doesn't make sense any longer because, in 1979, the Service started identifying hurricanes by both male and female names alternately: Alma, Bertram, Charlotte, Donald, Elaine, and so on. That's one small step for humankind. It's the right thing that those meteorological "evil spirits" not be exclusively female.

Tsunami blows in from the Japanese *tsu*, "harbor," and *nami*, "wave." Travel from the back of the word to the front, and you'll find the anagram I AM NUTS!

I truly hope that you're *sky high* and *on cloud nine*, meaning "in a state of high euphoria." This is a reference to the ten types of clouds defined in *International Cloud Atlas*, first published in 1896 and still in use. Cloud nine is a cumulonimbus cloud that can rise to the lofty height of 6.2 miles, as high as a cloud can be.

I also hope you won't feel that I'm *stealing your thunder*. In 1709, the English poet and playwright John Dennis quilled the tragedy *Appius and Virginia*, which turned out to be a tragic failure among critics and playgoers alike. The play bombed even though Dennis had invented for it a device that generated the roaring of thunder as part of the staging. Sadly, the play generated more thunder claps than hand claps.

Shortly after the premature closing of Dennis's play, William Shakespeare's tragedy *Macbeth* came to London. Dennis attended an early performance, where he heard his own thunder machine roar during the three witches' opening scene on the heath. The upstaged Dennis exclaimed, "By God! The villains will not play my play, but they will steal my thunder!" And that's where we get the expression steal my thunder, meaning "to be robbed of deserved glory."

All of us can take a lesson from the weather. It pays no attention to criticism. Now that you're getting acclimated to the concept of weather metaphors, complete each phrase with a word from the following weather words:

The Weather Chart

bolt	gale	slush
breeze	hail	snow
climate	hazy	storm
cloud	ice	sunny
cool	lightning	tempest
flood	misty	thunder
Fog	rain	whirlwind
frozen	shower	wind

1. _____s of laughter 2. _____ in a teapot 3. _____struck 4. greased _____ 5. _____ side up 6. a _____ from the blue

7. a _____ fund 8. a _____ job 9. a _____ tour 10. a _____ of emotions 11. _____ assets 12. shoot the _____

13. brain_____ 14. break the _____ 15. get _____ of 16. take a _____ check 17. my memory of the evening is _____ 18. I'm in a _____

19. on _____ nine 20. a _____ of bullets 21. _____ with praise 22. a _____ cat 23. _____-eyed 24. the _____ of opinion

Answers

1. gale 2. tempest 3. thunder 4. lightning 5. sunny 6. bolt
7. slush 8. snow 9. whirlwind 10. flood 11. frozen 12. breeze
13. storm 14. ice 15. wind 16. rain 17. hazy 18. fog
19. cloud 20. hail 21. shower 22. cool 23. misty 24. climate

Plane Talk

Two wrongs don't make a right, but two Wrights did make an airplane, and that invention has inspired the English language to fly up, up, and away. Don't go into a tailspin. Straighten up and fly right by the seat of the pants ("to fly by instinct rather than instruments") on a wing and a prayer, even if you take a lot of flak. *Flak*, which seems to echo the sound of anti-aircraft shells, is adopted from the German acronym *FLeigerAbwehrKanone*, literally "pilot defense cannon."

The popular phrase "pushing the envelope" does not mean "working at a post office." The expression came into general use following the publication of Tom Wolfe's mega-selling book about the space program, *The Right Stuff*: "One of the phrases that kept running through the conversation was 'pushing the outside of the envelope'... [That] seemed to be the great challenge and satisfaction of flight testing." Wolfe didn't originate the term, although it's appropriate that he used it in a technical and engineering context, as it was first used in the field of mathematics.

The envelope here is the mathematical envelope, the locus of the ultimate intersections of consecutive curves. That envelope describes the upper and lower limits of the various factors that it is safe to fly at, such as speed, engine power, maneuverability, wind velocity and altitude. By pushing the envelope, that is, challenging those limits, test pilots are able to determine just how far it was safe to go. The expression has now expanded beyond aeronautics to mean "to seek innovation, to stretch established limits."

Don't forget that no matter how much you push the envelope, it'll still remain stationery.

As Mohith Agadi has written, "There's only one job in this world that gives you an office in the sky; and that is pilot." Before modern instruments, a pilot flew a plane based on how it felt. For example, in fog or clouds, in the absence of instrumentation a pilot could tell whether the plane was climbing or diving by how heavy he felt in the seat. *Seat of the pants*, first documented in 1929, is the area where one sits, i.e. the buttocks. Hence, airmen and airwomen often *flew by the seat of their pants, on a wing and a prayer.*

An ancient Roman copper coin was called an *as*, which simply meant "one," or "a unit." This meaning of "one" ultimately evolved into *ace* as the highest card in a playing deck and, in tennis, winning a point with a single serve. This embedded meaning of "topnotch" explains why an expert pilot is called an *ace*.

Helicopters don't fly; they beat the air into submission. As humorist Dave Barry, my fellow Haverford College alumnus, has written, "The truth is that helicopters are nothing at all like cars. Scientists still have no idea what holds helicopters up. Whatever it is, it could stop at any moment."

These mishmashes of whirling parts that can rise up, up, and away often lighten their load by shedding their first four letters to become *copters* or their last six letters to become *helos*. Then they take flight in a sky of metaphor—*chopper, eggbeater, whirlybird, windmill, dragonfly, air bear,* and *stick buddy*. A recent metaphoric extension is the compound *helicopter parents*, which describes moms and dads who constantly hover above their children's lives and activities.

Please note that *fly by night*, as in "a fly-by-night business," is not an aviation expression. Here *fly* simply means "run away, flee" under cover of darkness. On the other wing, *fly by wire* is a fairly new term in aviation. Nowadays, the cockpit (named from the cramped arena of flying feathers where cockfights take place) controls on large aircraft aren't balled throttles but electronic devices that talk to electric motors in the wings and tail via digital circuitry. Hence, *fly by wire.*

Balls to the wall (no lawsuits, please!) is an aviation metaphor that means "an all-out effort." On airplanes, the handles controlling the throttle and the fuel mixture are often topped with ball-shaped grips. Pushing those grips forward, close to the front wall of the cockpit, increases the amount of fuel going to the engines and generates the highest possible speed. As some airborne jester wrote, "If you push the stick forward, the houses get bigger. If you pull the stick back, they get smaller. Unless you keep pulling the stick back. Then they get bigger again."

Racing with the Moon, Dancing with the Stars

So far in this thematic cluster, the sky's been the limit. Now let's soar up, up and away to outer space. There we'll discover words and phrases that are out of this world.

I'm over the moon about moon words. Have you ever wondered why the words *lunatic* and *lunar* begin with the same four letters? Etymology supplies the answer. *Lunatic* derives from *luna*, Latin for "moon," which when it is full, is said to render us daft—*moonstruck* and *loony*.

We keep time with the moon. *Monday* began as Old English for "moon day," and *month*, again from Old English, is the duration between full moons, the time it takes our lunar satellite to complete its voyage around our planet.

A *honeymoon* is an early harmony in any relationship, especially marriage. Here we come to the juncture of "honey" and the long-ago way of saying "month": *moon*. The first month of marriage is often the sweetest, but just when the moon is full and bright, it begins to wane as can sadly happen with matrimony.

The opportunity to read an explanation about the phrase *once in a blue moon* comes along once in a blue moon, when pigs fly and hell freezes over. A blue moon is the second full moon in a single month, a phenomenon that occurs, well, once in a blue moon. These bonus full moons present themselves on average once every 2.7 years. The expression has nothing to do with the actual color of the moon, but whenever certain natural conditions align, such as volcanic eruptions or titanic fires sending particles into the atmosphere, the moon can actually appear to be tinged with blue.

Some of us distill or drink *moonshine* ("illegal liquor") or babble *moonshine* ("nonsense"). Some of us *moonlight* with a second job that we perform at night. Others of us *moon* over a desired lover. Then there's that other verb *to moon*. I'll leave you to figure out how that act got its name.

Moving right along to another body part, that whitish crescent at the base of each of your fingernails (none on your toenails) actually has a name—*lunule* or *lunula,* French-Latin for "little moon."

Scientists got tired of watching the moon go around the earth for twenty-four hours. They decided to call it a day.

Have you ever dined at the restaurant on the moon? The food is great, but the place doesn't have any atmosphere.

After those moonstruck, loony jokes, let's go dancing with the stars, which eclipse the moon when it comes to the intensity of the light they shine upon English words. In an astronomical number of ways, the English language sees stars. We are so starstruck and starry-eyed that we call our stage, screen, and athletic celebrities stars. May this verbivorous book be a *lodestar* ("way" + "star"), a source of inspiration in your life. A lodestar is used in navigation to show the way.

A Latin word for "star" is *stella,* whence the adjective *stellar,* the noun *constellation,* and name *Stella.* Another starry Latin word part is *astrum,* a prolific root that gives us *aster* ("a flower with star-shaped petals"), *astrology* ("star study"), *astronomer* ("star arranger"), *asteroid* ("star form"), and *astronaut* ("star sailor"). An asterisk is a symbol that looks like a "little star." You may wish to dispute these celestial etymologies, but I think you'd be an asterisk it.

In William Shakespeare's *Julius Caesar,* Cassius warns that "the fault, dear Brutus, lies not in our stars, but in ourselves." Nevertheless, for centuries, people have believed that the stars and their heavenly positions govern events on earth. If the conjunction of the stars is not propitious, disaster will strike. Created from the Latin *dis*, "bad, against," and *astrum*, *disaster* literally means "against the stars"—ill-starred, star-crossed. In the ghostly opening scene of *Hamlet*, Horatio speaks of "stars with trains of fire and dews of blood, disasters in the sun."

Astrologers used to study the stars to see how their coming together at a person's birth would influence his or her future. *Desire* is star-spun from the Latin *de*, "from," + *sidus*, "star." The idea is that we wish for and desire fortunate outcomes that stream from our lucky stars. In the same constellation is *consider*, which radiates from the Latin *cum*, "with" + *sidera*, "stars." The first meaning of *consider* was "to examine stars together to gauge their effects on our fate."

The influence of the stars reposes even within the word *influence* itself. *Influence* originally meant a flowing or streaming from the stars of an ethereal fluid that acted upon the character and destiny of human beings.

The ancients also believed that the influence of a star generated the *dog days*, summer periods of triple *h* weather—hazy, hot, and humid. In the days of the Romans, the six or eight hottest weeks of the summer, roughly July through the first half of August, were known colloquially as *caniculares dies*, or "days of the dog." According to Roman lore, the dog star Sirius rose with and added its heat to the sun, making a hot time of the year even hotter.

Galaxy, a Greek through Latin word that describes ginormous, humongous clusters of stars, originally meant "milky," as in *lactose* and *lactic*. We call our galaxy the Milky Way.

Derived from Greek *ekkentros*, "out of the center," from *ek*, "out of" + *kentron*, "center," *eccentric* first appeared in English in 1551 as an astronomical term describing "a circle in which a heavenly body deviates from its center." Modern-day astronomers still use *eccentric* in that way.

Greek also bequeaths us *zodiakos,* "circle of little animals." *Zodiac* is the ancient Greek name for the heavenly belt of twelve signs believed to influence human behavior. The *zo* – in *zodiac* is related to the *zo* – in *zoo* and *zoology*—"life."

Truth be told, I'm a Gemini, so I don't believe in astrology.

☺When Metaphors Collide

In the cluster you've just read this book you saw how we figuratively compare an emotionally lacerating experience to how a farm harrow pulverizes the earth, how we liken the shape of a tulip to a turban, how we coalesce starting up a conversation with breaking ice, and how we equate the whitish crescent at the base of each of our fingernails with a little moon.

These comparisons are called metaphors. Metaphors are the cat's pajamas and the cat's meow. They help us break the ice, bury the hatchet, blow off steam, and raise the bar for what makes colorful language. Without metaphors, we're a day late and a dollar short, out in left field, up the creek without a paddle, skating on thin ice, and falling into hot water.

Unfortunately, the strength of the metaphor is also its weakness. Because they're used so often and because so many of them sound or seem so much alike, it's easy to accidentally jumble two of them together, even when you *aren't* a bubble off plumb and three sheets to the wind. Flying in the face of physics, two metaphors *can* occupy the same space at the same time.

Should you ever realize that you've promiscuously mixed your metaphors, don't feel as if you laid an egg, have egg on your face, or that you're walking on eggshells or are sucking eggs. After all, sometimes that's just the way the cookie falls where it may, as we see when metaphors collide. Every mixed-up metaphor that follows is genuine, certified, and authentic. I swear on a stack of dictionaries

When Metaphors Collide

that I have not concocted any of them. I hope that they will kindle in you a flood of laughter:

- She has a mind like a steel sieve.
- The sacred cows have come home to roost.
- The communist menace is a snake in the grass that is gnawing away at the foundation of our ship of state.
- She was a diva of such immense talent that, after she performed, there was seldom a dry seat in the house.
- He came through the experience smelling like a knight in shining armor.
- We are in a butt-ugly recession right now, but we are seeing light at the end of the tunnel.
- The bankers' pockets are bulging with the sweat of the honest working man.
- They're biting the hand of the goose that laid the golden egg.
- A virgin forest is a place where the hand of man has never set foot.
- My crew cut made my ears stick out like a sore thumb.
- She kept breaking through the glass ceiling and that ruffled some feathers. "There were too many people looking to throw darts," she said.
- The president hit the bull's eye on the nose.
- The media report violent events, which leads others to become violent. That leads to more reporting, which brings on still more violence. It's a vicious snowball.
- My mother literally worked like a Trojan horse to put me through college.
- They pulled the plug out from under me.
- Fish or get off the pot.
- Don't worry. I've got an ace up my hole.
- Let's jump off that bridge when we come to it.

- Don't count all your chickens in one basket.
- She's robbing Peter to pay the piper.
- He's up a tree without a paddle.
- Keep your ear to the grindstone.
- Sometimes you've gotta stick your neck out on a limb.

That's the whole kettle of fish in a nutshell. So let's grab the bull by the tail and look it directly in the eye. This isn't rocket surgery or brain science. When you boil it right down to brass tacks, it's best to avoid mixing up your metaphors.

Food For Thought

WE SAY A MOUTHFUL

As a devout Foodist, I'm pleased to serve you a bountiful banquet of culinary word origins.

Both our food and our language are peppered with salt. The ancients knew that salt was essential to a good diet, and centuries before artificial refrigeration, it was the only chemical that could preserve meat. Thus, a portion of the wages paid to Roman soldiers was "salt money," with which to buy salt, derived from the Latin, *sal*. This stipend came to be called a *salarium*, from which we acquire the word *salary*. A loyal and effective soldier was quite literally worth his salt.

Salt seasons not only the word *salary*, but also the words *salad*, *salsa, sausage,* and *salami*. You don't have to take my etymological explanations with a grain of salt. That is, you, who are the salt of the earth, don't need to sprinkle salt on my word stories to find them palatable. They're already worth their salt.

If you know where the Big Apple is, why don't you know where the Minneapolis?— which raises the question "Whence cometh the phrase *Big Apple*, referring to New York City?"

The first print citation shows up in 1921 in a regular racing column in the *New York Morning Telegraph* by one John Fitz Gerald, in which he used *big apple* to refer to the race tracks of New York. By 1924, Fitz Gerald had broadened the phrase to identify the city itself: "The Big Apple, the dream of every lad that ever threw a leg over a thoroughbred. There's only one Big Apple. That's New York."

The columnist wrote that he had first heard the phrase from two Black stable hands in New Orleans in 1920, for whom the *big apple* was their name for the New York racetracks—the big time, "the goal of every aspiring jockey and trainer."

The cakewalk was originally a nineteenth-century entertainment invented by African Americans in the antebellum South. It was intended to satirize the stiff ballroom promenades of White plantation owners, who favored the rigidly formal dances of European high society.

Cakewalking slaves lampooned these stuffy moves by accentuating their high kicks, bows, and imaginary hat doffings, mixing the cartoonish gestures together with traditional African steps. Likely unaware of the dance's derisive roots, the Whites often invited their slaves to participate in Sunday contests, to determine which dancers were most elegant and inventive. The winners would receive a piece of cake, a prize that became the dance's familiar name. Doesn't that just *take the cake*?

After Emancipation, the contest tradition continued in Black communities; the *Oxford English Dictionary* dates the widespread adoption of *cakewalk* to the late 1870s. It was around this time that the *cakewalk* came to mean "an easy task"—not because the dance was particularly simple to do but because of its languid pace and association with weekend leisure.

Close cousin to cake is pie. In days of yore, housewives often needed to scrimp, even on essentials. Whenever wheat was in short supply, the bottom crust of pies was made with rye meal. Wheat was used only for the *upper crust*. Soon *upper crust* entered everyday speech to mean "the socially select."

Eating humble pie has nothing etymologically to do with the word *humble*, "lowly." The dish was really *umble pie*, a pie stuffed with the chopped or minced part of an animal's "pluck"—the heart, lungs, liver, and other innards—especially of a deer. While the lord of the manor and the upper crust feasted on a delectable haunch of venison, the gamekeeper and other servants had to settle for edible viscera.

In the cake and pie family is bread. *Companion* derives from the Latin *com*, "together," and *panis*, "bread." You and I are companions who break the bread of language together. Breaking bread was an important ritual of welcome and hospitality. Hence, the word *company*.

That wage earners are called breadwinners reminds us of the importance of bread in medieval life. Not surprisingly, both *lord* and *lady* are well-bread words. *Lord* descends from the Old English *hlaf*, "loaf," + *weard*, "keeper," and *lady* from *hlaf*, "loaf," + *dige*, "kneader." *Pumpernickel* is etymologically baked from the German *pumpern*, "to break wind," + *Nickel*, "devil, demon, goblin." The idea is that those who eat the heavy, dark, hard-to-digest rye bread are liable to be smitten by a diabolical flatulence.

So here's a toast to all those flavorful metaphors that add spice to our English language. Does that use of *toast* relate etymologically to the familiar slice of heated bread? In a word, yes. In the days of Queen Elizabeth I and William Shakespeare, it was common practice to dip a piece of spiced toast into the bottom of one's tankard of ale or glass of sack (a bitter sherry) to improve the flavor and remove the impurities. The libation itself thus became "a toast," as did the gesture of drinking to another's health.

I offer a toast to you, my fellow wordaholic, logolept, and verbivore: "Here's champagne to our real friends, and real pain to our sham friends!" Thank you for being a real friend of our glorious, uproarious, victorious, courageous, outrageous, contagious, stupendous, tremendous, end-over-endous English language!

☺We Eat Our Words

Now it's time to nibble on a spicy, meaty, juicy topic that I know you'll savor and relish. I'm talking about a full plate, the whole enchilada—an overflowing smorgasbord.

Feast your eyes on the veritable banquet of mushrooming food expressions that grace the table of our English language and season our tongue. As we chew the fat about the food-filled phrases that are packed like sardines and sandwiched into our everyday conversations, I'll sweeten the pot with some tidbits of food for thought.

I know what's eating you. I've heard through the grapevine that you don't give a fig about me because you think I'm nutty as a fruitcake and have gone crackers and bananas; that you're fed up with me for biting off more than I can chew; that you want me to drop this subject like a hot potato because I'm a spoiled-rotten weenie in a pickle; and that you're giving me the raspberry for asking you to swallow a cheesy, corny, mushy, saccharine, seedy, soupy, sugar-coated, syrupy topic that just isn't your cup of tea.

Okay, so you're beet red with anger that I'm feeding you a bunch of baloney, garbage, and tripe; that I'm making you ruminate on a potboiler that's no more than a tempest in a teapot; that I've upset your apple cart by rehashing an old chestnut that's just pie in the sky and won't amount to a hill of beans; that you want to chew me out for buttering you up and putting words in your mouth; and that you're simmering because you think I'm an out-to-lunch bad apple who's out to egg you on.

But nuts to all that. That's the way the cookie crumbles. Eat your heart out and stop crying in your beer. I'm going to stop mincing words, start cooking with gas, take my idea off the back burner, and bring home the bacon without hamming it up. No matter how you slice it, this fruitful, tasteful topic is the icing on the cake and the greatest thing since sliced bread.

Rather than crying over spilt milk and leaping out of the frying pan into the fire, I'm going to put all my eggs in one basket, take potluck, and spill the beans. I'm cool as a cucumber and confident that this crackerjack, peachy-keen feast that I've cooked up will have you eating out of my hand.

I don't wish to become embroiled in a rhubarb, but your beefing and stewing sound like sour grapes from a tough nut to crack—kind of like the pot calling the kettle black. But if you've digested the spoon-fed culinary metaphors from this meat-and-potatoes and bread-and-butter narrative, the rest will be gravy, duck soup, a picnic, a cream puff, a can of corn, a piece of cake, and easy as pie—just like taking candy from a baby.

Hot dog! I hope you're happy that this souped-up topic is a plum, not a lemon, the berries, not the pits. For all the tea in China, this cream of the crop of palate-pleasing food figures is bound to sell like hotcakes. I'm no glutton for punishment, but if I'm wrong, I'll eat crow and humble pie.

For my language comedy they pay me a whole lot of bread, dough, cabbage, clams, and lettuce—not small potatoes, chicken-feed, or peanuts. I've lived beyond my salad days to a ripe old age, but I'm also a smart cookie who's feeling his oats and who's full of beans. I may be wrinkled as a prune, but I'm a salt-of-the-earth good egg who takes the cake, knows his onions, makes life a bowl of cherries, and is the apple of your eye and the toast of the town. As always, the proof of the pudding is in the eating.

So in a nutshell, it all boils down to the fact that every day we say a mouthful, and we truly eat our words.

😁Unappetizing Menus

- A Japanese restaurant cautions, "Menus Are for Eating Customers Only."
- A Swiss restaurant boasts, "Our Wines Leave You Nothing to Hope For."
- An Indian restaurant advertises, "We Serve Tea In a Bag Like Mother."
- A Shanghai Mongolian hot-pot buffet guarantees, "You Will Be Able to Eat All You Wish Until You are Fed Up."
- An establishment in Cairo assures patrons that "The Drinking Water in This Restaurant Has Been Passed By The Authorities."

Hungry? Here's a "full-coarse meal" I've put together consisting of skewed and skewered items spotted by tourists around the world. Bon appétit!

Soup – Cup $5 / Bowel $8
Gritty Balloons in Soup Barely Soup
Fisherman's Crap Soup
Soap of the Day
Limpid Red Beet Soup with Cheesy
Dumplings in the Form of a Finger

Salad
Salad, a Firm's Own Make
Groin Salad
Thai Style Uterus Salad

Unappetizing Menus

Meat
Buff Steak
Warm Little Dogs
Calf Pluck
Roast Beast
Sir Loin
Meat Dumping
Irritable Scalloped Kidney
Beef Rashers Beaten Up in the Country People's Fashion
Gut Casserole
Hambugger
Dreaded Veel Cutlets
Pork with Fresh Garbage
Liver Worst
Demonic Steak
Amiable and Sour Pork

Poultry
Chicken Low Mein
Hen Fried with Butler
Chicken in a Casket
Foul Breast
Frayed Chicken
Goose Barnacles
Chicken Pox Pie
Roasted Duck Let Loose
Utmost of Chicken Fried in Bother
Lightly Flowered Chicken Breast

Vegetables
Priest Fainted Eggplant
Muchrooms
Cabitch
Mushed Potatoes
Potato Cheeps

Sundries
Antipaste
Toes with Butter & Jam
Fried Hormones
Baked Zit
Mixed Boils to Pick
Muffled Frog Rumps
Fried Swarm
Spaghetti Fungoole
Gollum Shrimp
Drunken Prawns in Spit
Tortilla Topped with Melted Cheese,
Sour Cream and Glaucoma

Desserts
Lady's Finger
Strawberry Crap
Chocolate Sand Kooky
Tart of the House
Chocolate Mouse Tort
Chocolate Puke

Beverages
White Whine
Turkey Coffee
Special Cocktail for Women with Nuts

☺What's In a Name?

Here's a little test of your knowledge about food names.

French fries were invented in Belgium. *Frenching* simply describes a method of cutting vegetables into long strips. Danish pastry originated in Vienna, Austria, Swiss steak in England, Chinese gooseberries in New Zealand, Jordan almonds in Spain, and Jerusalem artichokes in North and South America—and they're tubers, not artichokes.

How are refried beans made? Despite the name, refried beans are not fried twice. *Frijoles refritos* actually means "well fried," not "refried."

There no ham in a hamburger, no butter in buttermilk, no egg in eggplant, no chocolate in white chocolate, and no straw in a strawberry. The strawberry is not a berry; but tomatoes, bananas, peppers, eggplant, kiwis, and watermelons are. A lychee nut is not a nut but a fruit of the soapberry family. A pineapple consists neither of pine nor apple. A peanut is neither a pea nor a nut. It's a legume. Welsh rabbit, often called Welsh rarebit, is a meatless dish whose primary ingredient is melted cheese. An egg cream contains neither eggs nor cream. Its ingredients are milk, chocolate syrup, and a jet of seltzer water. Shortbread is a thick cookie, and a sweetbread is not sweet and not bread. It's from a calf's or lamb's pancreas or thymus. And a doughnut hole is really a doughnut ball. The hole remains in the doughnut.

Taking Care of Business

ENGLISH MEANS BUSINESS

In bygone days, wandering peddlers were a familiar part of the American scene. An essential part of the peddlers' business was the buying and selling of gold. To test the value of gold, the peddler would file a shallow groove in the item he was considering and touch it with nitric acid. Color reactions from the acid would reveal the approximate gold content, and inferior metals would be decomposed by the treatment. This procedure was known as the *acid test*; and by extension, any exacting method designed to reveal hidden flaws has come to be known by this term.

Another golden word is *touchstone*, a criterion or standard, whose meaning goes straight back to goldsmiths, who kept hard stones, usually jasper or basalt, in their shops. When a customer brought in some gold, the goldsmith would rub it against the stone. With his practiced eye, the goldsmith could determine from the streak left on the stone the purity and quality of the gold. Hence, *touchstone*.

Business started out as a general term meaning literally "busy-ness." After several centuries of life, *business* picked up the narrower meaning of "commercial dealings." In 1925 Calvin Coolidge used the word in both its generalized and specialized senses when he stated, "The chief business of the American people is business." We today can see the word starting to generalize back to its first meaning in phrases like "I don't like this funny business one bit."

To the ledger of words once reserved for business alone we can add a number of products now shared in our common language:

I hope you feel that I'm *getting down to brass tacks* about business English. The popular explanation is that, in the past, dry goods stores, brass tacks were driven into the sales counters to mark a quarter-, half-, and full yard. Rather than holding up a bolt of piece goods and guessing the measurement, merchants would lay the swath on the counter and calculate accurately by *getting down to brass tacks*. Some language detectives lean toward *brass tacks* as cockney rhyming slang for *facts*.

Grocers of bygone days used a long pole or mechanical grabber (invented by Benjamin Franklin, by the way) to tip a can on a high shelf or at the top of a pile. The can would tumble into the grocer's waiting hands or open apron, just as a soft fly ball settles easily into a fielder's glove. Thus, a languid fly ball in baseball is dubbed *a can of corn*.

In the days of hand typesetting, the terms *upper case* and *lower case* originated from the way that type—individual letters that were cast from metal alloys—were stored. The type was sorted by letter and kept in specially designed wooden or metal cases, with separate cases for capital and small letters. The case containing the capital letters—"the upper case"—was placed on a rack above the case housing the small, and more frequently used, letters—"the lower case."

Cliché comes to us from the Old French *cliquer*, "to click." That's the sound printers used to make when they took a wood engraving and struck it into molten lead to make a cast. This mold was a *stereotype*, from the Greek *stereos*, "solid," which was used to reproduce a picture over and over. Hence, the metaphorical stereotype, which forms a fixed, unchangeable image in the mind's eye.

Clichés begin their lives as imaginative expressions and comparisons. That's how they become clichés. Like a phonograph needle, our words settle into the grooves that the clichés have worn into our speech and writing. Phrases that once possessed power become trite, hackneyed, and lifeless—adjectives that themselves are clichés for clichés.

A student wrote in an essay, "The boy came back from recess with a cliché on his face."

"A cliché on his face? Whatever do you mean?" asked the teacher.

"A cliché!" the student answered. "You know, a worn-out expression."

Using clichés is as easy as ABC, one-two – three, pie, falling off a log, shooting fish in a barrel, and taking candy from a baby. They make us happy as a clam, a lark, a kid in a candy shop, and a pig in, um, slop.

But if you want to hit the bull's eye, the spot, the jackpot, the lottery, the ground running, the ball out of the park, and the nail on the head, then you should be able to avoid clichés like the plague.

Certain herbs sold in herbalists' shops were prepared ahead of time and thus lacked the freshness of herbs newly picked. Since the early eighteenth century, these herbs have been labeled *cut and dried*. It's easy to see how that phrase came to signify anything boring and lacking in spontaneity.

In the phrase *dead as a doornail*, what's so dead about a doornail? To find out, we must look back through the centuries to the craft of carpentry. Long-ago carpenters drove bigheaded metal nails into doors to connect the crosspieces on the back. The carpenters would hook the tip of the nail back to "clinch" the nail (as we clinch a deal). The nail was "dead," meaning "fixed, rigid, immovable," as in *deadline* and *deadlock*. Carpenters today still use the term "deadnailing." It didn't take long for the pun on "fixed, rigid, immovable" and "not alive" to become clinched in our language, as in Charles Dickens's opening in *A Christmas Carol*: "Old Marley was as dead as a door-nail."

The adjective *normal* hails from Latin *normalis*, "a carpenter's square." This handy tool could ensure that your walls were at solid right angles and that all parts of a structure were even and balanced, i.e. *all squared away* and *on the level*.

We strive *to make ends meet.* What are the ends, and how do they meet? The phrase was originally a nineteenth-century bookkeeping term. The bookkeeper's task was, and still is, to make both ends ("assets and liabilities") meet ("equal, balance"). There's no accounting for taste, and, as for me, I have no taste for accounting.

Commercial life in medieval times was organized by guilds. An English apprentice who wished to be recognized as a master, with the right to work without supervision, was required to submit an article of metal, wood, stone, or leather, depending on his guild. Like today's academic dissertations, the quality of the work determined the artisan's future, and it came to be known as a *master piece.*

At one time, elaborate hats were a feature of everyday fashion. The people who made those hats were called hatters. They often used mercury to felt the animal fur they worked, but mercury had the side effect of making hatters go insane. The technical term for this illness is *erethism,* but the popular phrase is *mad as a hatter.*

The noun *context* is borrowed from the Latin *contexere,* "to weave together." While many fabrics are colored or printed after they are woven, wool is sometimes dyed before it's woven into cloth. The color of that wool is through-and-through and impossible to remove completely. So when we say someone is a "dyed-in-the-wool" conservative, liberal, environmentalist, animal-rights supporter, Yankees fan, etc., we mean that their beliefs are steadfast and permanent.

Textiles are also woven into the word *spinster* (*spin* + *ster,* "woman who"), "a woman who spins cloth" and unhappily has come to designate "an older woman who remains unmarried." Mercifully, this word is dying out, along with the card game called Old Maid. Some spinsters worked with a distaff, a short staff that held a bundle of fibers, flax, or wool that were twisted into yarn or thread. Over time, *distaff* has become a figure of speech for "womankind," female descent." The opposite of *distaff* (perhaps Freudianly) is *sword side* or *spear side.*

When people say they feel they've been *put through the mill,* they echo a metaphor from the trade of milling. Grain fed to the jaws of a great stone mill is subjected to heavy and thorough grinding. By figurative extension, any person receiving rough treatment is said to be *put through the mill*. Related words and expressions include *milling around, run-of-the-mill,* and *millstone*, the circular stone used for grinding, but now meaning "a heavy burden."

I'll bet you've wondered what the heck is the whack that someone or something is out of in the vogue phrase *out of whack*. Wonder no more. The most likely source is the auctioneer's hammer, which, when whacked, signals the conclusion of a competitive purchase. Without that final whack, all is discombobulated, catawampus—out of whack. Out of *whack* bears some resemblance to *waiting for the other shoe to drop*. You're trying to fall asleep in a hotel room when you hear the thud of a shoe hitting the floor in the next room. You lie awake for hours waiting for the other shoe to drop.

Fighting Words

Have you heard about these Knights of the Round Table?:

- Sir Cumference, the roundest Knight at the Round Table;
- Sir Loin, the rarest of the knights;
- Sir Cumcision, who always cut people off;
- Sir Prize, who always came up with something new;
- Sir Cus, the foul-mouthed clown;
- Sir Mount, the brave knight;
- Sir Render, the cowardly knight;
- Sir Rendipitous, who stumbled upon the Holy Grail by sheer luck;
- Sir Press, the royal censor;
- Sir Amic, who had feet of clay;
- Sir Real, the otherworldly knight;
- Sir Plus, the over-the-top knight;
- Sir Reptitious, the secretive knight who always repeated himself;
- Sir Charge and Sir Tax, the capitalists;
- and Sir Lee, the teenage knight.

Knight is a word that has come up in the world. Descended from the Anglo – Saxon *cnicht* (sounded as two syllables), *knight* evolved from meaning "a boy" to "a servant," and, finally, "a servant of a noble." I am a freelance writer of magazine and newspaper pieces. That means that I write these articles on a fee-paid assignment basis rather than on a regular-salary basis for a single employer. Most medieval knights were committed to a feudal lord, but those who weren't could hire themselves and their lances to anyone willing to pay for their "freelance" military services. The word *freelance* is one of Sir Walter Scott's myriad word inventions, appearing first in his celebrated novel *Ivanhoe* (1820).

Writers, students, workers, and business people constantly face *deadlines*, dates when manuscripts homework, and reports must be submitted and orders filled. When such deadlines are not met, penalties result, such as lower grades or loss of business. But the punishment for passing beyond the original deadlines was more deadly.

During the American Civil War, a deadline was a line of demarcation around the inner stockade of a prison camp, generally about seventeen feet. At the notorious Confederate camp in Andersonville, Georgia, a line was actually marked out some distance from the outer wire fence. Any prisoner crossing this line was shot on sight.

Writer Douglas Adams quips, "I love deadlines. I like the whooshing sound they make as they fly by."

Most writers hope to create a *blockbuster*. That bombshell of a word originated in World War II Britain as Royal Air Force slang for a bomb of enough penetrating power to shatter whole blocks of homes and pavements. By the late 1940s *blockbuster* had come to signify a megahit play, film or book.

If adults commit adultery, do infants commit infantry? Chuckle chuckle, snort snort!— but we are led to ask what is the relationship, if any, between infants and *infantry*? *Infant* was born from the Latin *in-*, "not" + *fari*, "speak" = "one who is not yet capable of speech." In Italian, *infante* came to mean "boy" or "foot soldier"; hence, our word *infantry*.

A fancy synonym for the adjective *drunk* is *intoxicated*. The Greek word *toxon* meant "bow" (as in "arrow launcher"), and the poison Greek warriors used to tip their arrows took on the name *toxikon*. Thus, the first people to be intoxicated were those pierced by lethal arrows. Ultimately that poison became embedded in our word *intoxicate*, having traveled from the Greek military through late Latin *intoxicatus* to the drunken fellow who slurs, "Name your poison." Over time, *intoxicated* took on the figurative sense of "to excite or elate to the point of enthusiasm or frenzy."

War, humanity's most destructive enterprise, is also among its most productive when it comes to generating new language. Because warfare has been a depressingly constant feature of our history, many of our words, expressions, and metaphors are of bellicose descent. *Freelance, deadline,* and *blockbuster* are but three such words among thousands that have entered our language through warfare and other hostilities. Here march some more fighting words, ones that start with the letters *A* to *G*:

Ambulance issues from an invention of Napoleon Bonaparte's *l'hôpital ambulant* ("walking hospital"), a light litter that served as a field hospital for wounded soldiers. We see the word *amble* in the Preamble to our Constitution, an initial walk before the longer journey through the document.

Assassin descends from the Arabic *hashshashin,* literally "hashish eaters." The original hashshashin were members of a religious and military order located in the mountains of Lebanon. These fanatics would commit political murder after being intoxicated with great quantities of hashish.

During World War I, *AWOL,* meaning "Absent Without Official Leave," was pronounced as four distinct letters. During World War II, *AWOL* was sounded as a single word, and the meaning was extended to civilian life to identify any person absent from any job or activity without explanation.

The 1960s expression *bang for the buck* began as a frivolous iteration for how much destructive power the Defense Department gets for the money it pays.

Figuratively, a *battle-ax* is a pejorative expression for a woman, often elderly, who is unpleasantly loud and aggressive. The original battle-ax was a sharp, broad ax used by Gothic tribes. When wielded or thrown, the weapon could penetrate Roman armor and split a shield

FIGHTING WORDS

Visit a Revolutionary War battle site such as Fort Ticonderoga, and you may see some gruesome artifacts in its museum—bullets with teeth marks in them. Possessing no real anesthesia to ease the agony of amputation, long-ago surgeons offered wounded soldiers the only pain reducer they could—a bullet to bite hard on. Just thinking about such trauma is enough to make me *sweat bullets*. After anesthesia was introduced in the United States in 1844, the expression *bite the bullet* came figuratively to mean "to deal with a stressful situation resolutely," as in Rudyard Kipling's lines:

Bite the bullet, old man,
And don't let them think you're afraid.

After the Norman Conquest of England in A.D. 1066, William the Conqueror required civilians to extinguish all fires and candles and stay inside after dark. Night patrols enforced this regulation by calling out "*Couvre feu!*" ("cover the fire"), which became *curfew* in English.

A *cohort* was a Roman military unit, composed of one tenth of a Roman legion.

An *emeritus* was originally a Roman soldier who had completed his term of service (Latin *emereor*, "obtain by service") and earned his discharge. Nowadays emeritus refers to retired professors, clergymen, and other retired officials.

A flash in the pan sounds as if it derives from the way prospectors pan rivers for gold. In truth, though, *a flash in the pan* refers to the occasional misfiring of the old flintlock muskets when the flash of the primer in the pan of the rifle failed to ignite the explosion of the charge. It is estimated that such misfirings ran as high as fifteen percent, leading *a flash in the pan* to come to mean "an intense but short-lived success or a person who fails to live up to their early promise."

Since the eighteenth century, *field day* has designated a special day set aside for military maneuvers and reviews. Through a linguistic process called expansion, *field day* has broadened to mean "a day marked by a sense of occasion and great success."

Muzzle loaders, then as now, had a half cock, or safety position, for a gun's hammer that back-locked the trigger mechanism so that the weapon couldn't be fired. The half-cock position doesn't generate enough power to make sparks to fire the pistol, so when a person *goes off half-cocked*, they are not in control of the situation.

The theory you've most likely heard that explains the birth of *gringo* is that U.S. troops marching off to the Mexican-American War (1846–48) lustily sang, "Green Grow the Rushes-O," prompting the Mexicans to construct *gringo* from the first two words of the title. In truth, *gringo* inhabited the Spanish vocabulary since the early eighteenth century, long before the Mexican-American conflict. Just as we say, "It's all Greek to me," Spanish speakers said, *hablar en griego,* "to speak in Greek," meaning "to speak in an unintelligible foreign tongue." It didn't take long for *griego* to morph into *gringo*.

What's My Line?

The verb *to vet* means "to examine credentials, manuscripts, or other documents as a veterinarian examines an animal, hoping to give it a clean bill of health." The noun *veterinarian* came about because the first veterinarians treated only animals that were old (Latin *vetus*) and experienced enough to perform work such as pulling a plow or hauling military baggage. That's why *veteran* and *veterinarian* start with almost the same letters.

Most occupational titles are self-explanatory: A teacher teaches, a preacher preaches, a gardener gardens, and a writer writes. But the origins of some job names are more obscure. *Veterinarian* is one example. *Janitor* is another, deriving from the Roman god Janus, who guarded doorways and gates. Close kin to *janitor* is *usher*, which has a long history, going all the way back to the Latin *ostium*, "door," related to *os*, "mouth," because a door was likened to the mouth of a building. *Usher*, then, turns out to be a body metaphor for a person who stands at a door.

A *professor* is "one who makes public declarations," while the first *deans* were military officers in charge of ten (*decem*) soldiers. Those *soldiers* were so called because they were paid in Roman coins called *solidi*.

A ventriloquist is someone who is skilled in the art of throwing his or her voice so that it appears to emanate from a source other than the speaker. Appropriately, the roots of *ventriloquist* are the Latin *ventris*, "belly" + *loqui*, "speaker." In other words, a ventriloquist is a "belly speaker." (I'm thinking of one day writing a book titled *Ventriloquism For Dummies*.)

The standard explanation traces *cop* or *copper*, meaning "police," to copper buttons worn on early police uniforms, or to copper police badges supposedly issued in some cities, but there is no convincing evidence for this conjecture.

Another theory explains *cop* as an acronym standing for "constable on patrol" or "chief of police." But these acronymic etymologies almost always turn out to be spurious, after-the-fact explanations. Another inconvenient truth is that acronyms were virtually unknown in English before the twentieth century, while *cop* itself was well-established by the mid-nineteenth century.

In reality, the law enforcement sense of *cop* and *copper* harks back to the Latin word *capere,* meaning "to seize," which also gives us *capture*. *Cop* as a slang term meaning "to catch, snatch, or grab" took its place in English in the eighteenth century. Criminals apprehended by the police were said to have been "copped"—caught by the "coppers" or "cops."

Why are psychiatrists often called shrinks? After all, psychiatry seeks to expand people's self-knowledge, abilities, and options, not to shrink them. Turns out that the slang term *shrink* applied to those who practice psychotherapy is a shortened form of *headshrinker,* a jocular comparison to primitive peoples who dry and shrink the heads of their slain enemies.

When Geoffrey Chaucer quilled in his Prologue to *The Canterbury Tales*, "a clerk ther was of Oxenford," the poet was referring to a clergyman or cleric, the first meaning of the word *clerk*. In the Middle Ages, literacy was largely confined to the clergy, but *clerk* gradually became the name for bookkeepers, secretaries, and notaries—anyone who could read or write.

During the 1930s, when alarm clocks were expensive and unreliable, professional knocker uppers (generally women) were people entrusted to wake up workers. The knocker uppers earned about six pence a week shooting dried peas out of peashooters at the windows of sleeping workers in East London. They would not move on until they were certain that the laborer had awakened.

Now have a look at a passage from *The Octopus* (1901), by American novelist Frank Norris:

> Lyman Derrick sat dictating letters to his typewriter.
> "That's all for the present," he said at length.
> Without reply, the typewriter rose and withdrew, thrusting her pencil into the coil of her hair, closing the door behind her, softly, discreetly.

Norris was not fabricating a science-fiction tale featuring robot typewriters. Rather, back in the late nineteenth and early twentieth century, a typewriter was a person who worked on a typewriting machine, not the machine itself.

Have you ever worried about the fact that the person with whom you trust your hard-earned life savings is called a *broker*? Worry no more: The original broker was one who broaches (opens) casks of wine.

The surname *Webber* means "a man who weaves," *Webster* "a woman who weaves." *Brewer* signifies "a man who brews," *Brewster* "a woman who brews." *Dyer* is the last name of "a man who dyes cloth," *Dexter* the last name of "a woman who dyes cloth." *Baker*, of course, denotes "a man who bakes," while *Baxter* denotes "a woman who bakes."

Here's an inventory of additional vocational names and their not-so-apparent origins:

- *bursar*. one who controls the purse (*bursa*)
- *chauffeur*. one who stokes the fires of the engine in a steam-driven car
- *constable*. one who tended his lord's horses and stables
- *coroner*. an officer of the crown (*corona*)

- *diplomat.* one who vets and carries an official state document (related to *diploma*)
- *grocer.* one who sells by the gross
- *manufacturer.* one who makes products by hand (Latin *manus*, "hand" + *facere*, "perform.")
- *nurse.* one who nourishes
- *orthopedist.* one who corrects (the bones of) children
- *pastor.* a spiritual herdsman
- *plumber.* one who works with lead (*plumbum*)
- *restaurateur.* one who works at a place where patrons are restored
- *secretary.* one to whom secrets are entrusted
- *sheriff.* a stitching together of Old English *shire*, "county," and *reeve*, "local administrator"
- *surgeon.* one who works with his hands
- *vicar.* substitute for God (*vicarious*).
- *whitesmith.* A blacksmith forges iron; a whitesmith works with tin.

Coining Phrases

Money makes the world go around. It also makes our language go around. Not only does money talk. We talk about money.

To coin a phrase, I'm not a guy who's phony as a three dollar bill and not worth a red cent or a plugged nickel. I'm not penny wise and pound foolish, and I won't short change you. Dollars to doughnuts, I'm not a day late and a dollar short, and I won't nickel and dime you to death. If you don't give me your two cents, I'll give you a penny for your thoughts.

We also make jokes about money:

- You look like a million dollars—all green and wrinkled.
- Have you heard about the couple who spent $250,000 on their son's college education—and all they got was a quarterback?
- Do you want to get rich? Simply purchase fifty female pigs and fifty male deer—and you'll have a hundred sows and bucks.

Now I'm going to put my money where my mouth is. I'm also going to put my mouth where the money is. That's why they pay me the big bucks.

Most of us consider a talent to be a gift that has little to do with money. But in ancient times a talent was a unit of weight in silver or gold that functioned as a monetary unit, one that figures prominently in Jesus's parable of the talents (Matthew 25: 14-15): "For the kingdom of heaven is as a man traveling in a far country, who called his own servants and delivered unto them his goods. And unto one he gave five talents, to another two and to another one, to every man according to his several ability." The current meaning of *talent*, some special, often God-given ability or aptitude, is a figurative extension of the parable.

What about the ubiquitous financial metaphor *scot-free*? The compound has nothing to do with Scotland or the Scottish people. Even before Shakespeare's day, a scot was a municipal tax paid to a sheriff or bailiff. So for centuries those who got off scot-free managed to avoid paying their taxes. Their progeny still walk the earth.

A *picayune* was originally a Spanish half real (pronounced "ray-ahl") worth about six cents and circulated throughout the American South. It didn't take long for prices to rise and for inflation to erode the already paltry value of the coin. Up grew the phrase "not worth a picayune," referring to something of little value. Before long, *to be picayune* about a matter came to mean to be petty or picky.

Here's a quiz that's right on the money. Fill in each blank with a monetary term.

1. Don't take any wooden _____.
2. Two bits, four bits, six bits, a _____!
3. Don't pass the _____.
4. You can bet your bottom _____.
5. Stop on a _____.
6. My stamp collection is in _____ condition.

The answers are *nickels, dollar, buck, dollar, dime,* and *mint*. Whence the wooden nickel in the first poser? During the centennial celebration of the United States, in Philadelphia, commemorative tokens made of wood sold for five cents each. These coins were accepted as legal tender while the festivities were in progress; but, of course, they ceased to have value after the show was over. So beginning in the last part of the nineteenth century, the advice *Don't take any wooden nickels* became the popular equivalent of "Don't be a sucker."

Coining Phrases

Why do two bits equal a quarter, four bits a half dollar, and six bits seventy-five cents? Because early in our nation's history, Mexican currency was used interchangeably with local coinage, and the Spanish real ("re-AHL"), a coin worth twelve – and-a-half cents, was called a bit. When the U.S. quarter dollar piece was minted, it quickly acquired the slang label *two bits*.

Why *mint condition*? The compound originally referred to coins that were never put into circulation and thus remained in the same pristine state as when they were produced at the mint. *Mint condition* has broadened to describe "a state of being like new," whether it be stamps, comic books, baseball cards, and the like.

You can *bank on* my expertise; *it's like money in the bank*, and *you can take it to the bank*. No longer will you be *penny wise and pound foolish* and unable *to make head nor tail* of expressions such as *don't take any wooden nickels*.

☺You're Fired!

The meaning of *fired*, "to discharge someone from a job," is an extension of applying fire to gunpowder. But nobody gets fired anymore. How do I fire thee? Let me count the ways. Euphemisms for getting bounced include *decruited, deselected, destaffed, downsized, excessed, indefinite idling, negotiated departure, nonpositively terminated, nonretained, outplaced, premature retirement, reclassified, redundancy elimination, RIF (reduction in force), vocational relocation, involuntary normal attrition,* and (gasp!) *workforce imbalance correction.*

I powerfully doubt that such corporate doublespeak assuages the workers, who knew they are really being *fired, axed, bounced, canned, eighty-sixed, laid off, let go, sacked, shown the door,* and *given the old heave-ho.*

In the continuing search for newer, softer, and more ambiguous verbs with which to administer the final blow to helpless jobholders, Laurence Urdang, the late editor of the late *Verbatim, the Language Quarterly,* came up with a sparkling new pun game:

If clergymen are defrocked and lawyers are disbarred, then alcoholics are delivered, hairdressers are distressed, manicurists are defiled, models are disposed, and pornographers are deluded.

Employing the *de –* and *dis –* prefixes, I offer my own multiple verbs for getting rid of members of other professions:

- Bankers are distrusted and disinterested.
- Cowboys are debunked, deranged, and decaffeinated.
- Elks Clubbers are dislodged and dismembered.
- Judges are disrobed, dishonored, disappointed, and defined.

You're Fired!

- Magicians are dispelled and disillusioned.
- Mathematicians are deciphered, disfigured, discounted, and dissolved.
- Preachers are demoralized, decreed, distracted, and dissected.
- Songwriters are denoted and decomposed.
- Tailors are depressed, depleted, and dispatched.
- Teachers are declassified, detested, and degraded.
- Tennis players are deduced, disadvantaged, deserved, and defaulted.

The Hello Name Game

These days, we often attend conferences, parties, and other gatherings where we are asked to wear name tags that say, "Hello, My Name is ____." The beloved humorist Erma Bombeck tells this story: "A member of the committee slapped a name tag over my left bosom. 'What shall we name the other one?' I smiled. She was not amused."

Here's a punderful game that takes those badges to the limit. The object is to match a real first name with a real profession to spark a punny connection, as in "My name is Lorrie, and I'm a trucker," "My name is Ophelia, and I'm a masseuse," and "My name is Tyler, and I design bathrooms."

Hello, our names are…
- Abbott, Abby, Angel, Charity, Chastity, Christian, Faith, Glory, Grace, Hope, Mercy, Neal, and Temple, and we're servants of the church.
- Ace, Bette, Chip, and Delia, and we work in a casino.
- Alexis, Axel, Cab, Carmen, Chevy, Jack, Mercedes, Otto, Phillip, Portia, and Van, and we work on cars.
- Amber, Crystal, Goldie, Jade, Jasper, Jules, Opal, Pearl, Ring, Ruby, and Sapphire, and we're jewelers.
- Annette, Bob, Brooke, Doc, Eddie, Finn, Gil, Marina, Marlon, Piers, Rod, and Rowan, and we're fisherpeople.
- April, August, January, June, May, Summer, and Tuesday, and we make calendars.
- Art, Dot, Drew, Garrett, and Hugh, and we're painters.

The Hello Name Game

- Arthur and Page, and we're writers.
- Avery, Crane, Jay, Martin, Raven, Rhea, Robin, and Wren, and we're ornithologists.
- Barney and Timothy, and we're farmers.
- Baron, Duke, Earl, Gaylord, and King, and we're noblemen.
- Barry, Di, Doug, and Paul, and we're undertakers.
- Basil, Blanche, Eaton, Ginger, Herb, Rosemary, and Sage, and we're chefs.
- Bea, Buzz, Honey, Ladybird, Midge, and Nat, and we're entomologists.
- Belle and Isabel, and we play the carillon.
- Bertha, Spike, and Ty, and we work on a railroad.
- Bill, Buck, and Penny, and we work at the mint.
- Billy and Nanny, and we herd goats.
- Bing, Cherry, Melanie, and Peaches, and we sell fruit.
- Blossom, Bud, Dahlia, Daisy, Fern, Flora, Heather, Holly, Iris, Ivy, Jasmine, Lily, Pansy, Pete, Petunia, Posey, Rose, and Violet, and we're horticulturalists.
- Branch, Forest, Hazel, Hugh, Leif, Magnolia, Myrtle, Twiggy, and Woody, and we're arborists.
- Brandy, Margarita, Olive, and Sherry, and we're bartenders.
- Buffy, Fanny, Lena, Les, and Skip, and we're weight-loss counselors.
- Bunny and Warren, and we raise rabbits.
- Candy, Carmela, Lolly, and Sugar, and we're confectioners.
- Celeste, Jupiter, Sky, Starr, and Venus, and we're astronomers.
- Chick and Henny, and we raise poultry.
- Chuck, Frank, Ham, and Stu, and we're butchers.
- CiCi, Iris, and Seymour, we're opticians.
- Claude and Rory, and we're lion tamers.
- Cliff, Craig, and Rocky, and we're mountaineers.
- Colt and Winnie, and we train horses.
- Dale, Glen, and Heath, and we sell country real estate.
- Dawn, Dewey, Gail, Hale, Misty, Sky, Storm, and Sunny, and we're meteorologists.

- Emory, Hans, and Philo, and we're manicurists.
- Flip and Patty, and we cook hamburgers.
- Flo, John, Lou, Lulu, and Piper, and we're plumbers.
- Hank and Harry, and we're barbers.
- Harmony, Harper, Lute, Melody, and Viola, and we're musicians.
- Helmut, Lance, and Pierce, and we're knights.
- Holly and Noel, and we sell Christmas plants.
- Hunter and Lionel, and we lead safaris.
- Ira and Rich, and we're investment advisers.
- Jose and Smoky, and we're firefighters.
- Josh, Smiley, and Whit, and we're comedians.
- Kitty, Tabby, and Tom, and we raise cats.
- Lacey, Levi, Serge, and Taylor, and we sell clothing.
- Laurel, Vi, Victor, and Wynne, and we're Olympic champions.
- Michelle, Sandy, Shelly, and Wade, and we're lifeguards at the beach.
- Rex and Rusty, and we own a junkyard.
- Sue and Will, and we're lawyers.

☺Nothing Works for Me

Some people hold the same job for their entire career. Others move from one job to another while relentlessly ascending the corporate ladder. My personal workplace history is more checkered:

- My first job was working in an orange juice factory, but I couldn't concentrate, so I got canned.
- Then I became a lumberjack, but I just couldn't hack it, so they gave me the axe.
- I was once a set designer, but I left without making a scene.
- I was next employed at a diet center, but I got downsized.
- I became a baker, but I turned out to be a loafer and couldn't make enough dough.
- Then I opened a donut shop, but I soon got tired of the hole business.
- I manufactured calendars, but my days were numbered.
- After that, I tried to be a tailor, but I just wasn't suited for it, because it was a sew-sew job, depleating, and de-pressing.
- I took a job as an upholsterer, but I never recovered.
- Next, I worked in a muffler factory, but that was exhausting.
- I became a hairdresser, but the job was just too cut-and-dried.
- I moved on to selling lingerie, but they decided to give me a pink slip.
- I tried telemarketing, but I had too many hang-ups.
- I manned a computer but developed a terminal illness and lost my drive and my memory.

- I became a dentist, but gummed up the works and couldn't do the drill. The job was boring and felt like a bridge to nowhere.
- I worked as a fortune-teller, but I didn't see any future in it.
- I sold origami, but the business folded.
- For a while, I was an astrologer, but it wasn't in the stars.
- Then I tried to be a chef. I figured it would add a little spice to my life, but I just didn't have the thyme, it didn't pan out, and my goose was cooked.
- I attempted to be a deli worker, but any way I sliced it, I couldn't cut the mustard.
- I studied a long time to become a doctor, but I didn't have the patients.
- I became a cardiologist, but my heart just wasn't in it.
- I took a job at UPS, but I couldn't express myself.
- Next was a job in a shoe factory, but the job didn't last and I got the boot.
- I studied to become a lawyer, but my career was brief. It was too trying and had no appeal.
- I tried selling vacuum cleaners, but the job really sucked.
- I became a Velcro salesman but couldn't stick with it.
- I was a commercial fisherman, but I missed the boat and discovered that I couldn't tackle the job and live on my net income.
- I was a masseur for a while, but I rubbed people the wrong way.
- I was once a photographer, but I never developed. It was a negative experience, and I hated the hot flashes.
- I became a Hawaiian garland maker, but I got leid off.
- I was a printer for a while, but I wasn't the type for the job, and I didn't have an inkling about what to do.
- I tried being a fireman, but I suffered burnout, so I couldn't climb my way to the top.
- I wanted to be a banker, but I wasn't ready to make a change. I lacked interest and maturity so I withdrew from consideration.

Nothing Works For Me

- I got a job at a zoo feeding giraffes, but I was fired because I wasn't up to it.
- So then I became a personal trainer in a gym, but they said I wasn't fit for the job.
- I tried selling cigarette lighters, but I lost my spark.
- Next, I found being an electrician interesting, but I had to strip to make ends meet. I wasn't emotionally grounded and the work was shocking and revolting, so they discharged me.
- I thought that becoming a tennis pro would yield a net gain, but it wasn't my kind of racket. I was too high-strung and didn't have any love for the game.
- I tried being a teacher, but I soon lost my principal, my faculties, and my class.
- I trained to be a ballet dancer, but I was seldom on point and it was too-too difficult.
- For a while, I was a farmer, but problems cropped up and I wasn't outstanding in my field.
- I took the plunge as a plumber, but it turned out to be a pipe dream. I was out of sink, so the job went down the drain.
- I worked as an elevator operator. The job had its ups and downs. I got the shaft and took steps to quit.
- I applied for a job at an Air & Space Museum, but there was nothing inside.
- I thought about becoming a poet, but the work was a verse to my being. Iamb what iamb.
- I sold chocolate ice cream, diced marshmallows, and nuts, but the job became a rocky road.
- I became a candle maker. At first business waxed strong. Then it tapered off.
- My first day on the snow job as a ski instructor I slipped up, and it was all downhill from there.
- I did a stint in a pizza shop. I kneaded the dough, but my pies were too cheesy.

- I took a job as a cook in a monastery as both the fish friar and the chip monk. I tried to communicate with the clergy, but they excommunicated me.
- I once worked as an optometrist. The future looked clear, and my life was coming into focus. Then I got too close to the lens grinder and made a spectacle of myself.
- I tried cleaning pools, but I went into the tank and was out of my depth.
- I worked at an unemployment agency. Even when they fired me. I still had to go in.
- I became a statistician, but I got broken down by age, sex, and marital status.
- I was once a Scrabble champion, but I became inconsonant, and I can't move my vowels anymore. My next trip to the bathroom could spell disaster!

So I've retired, and I find that I'm perfect for this job!

Sports Illustrated

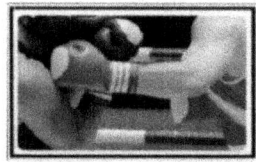

Our Sporty English Language

Sometimes it seems that almost all Americans either play sports or watch them. Because competition occupies such a central place in American life and imagination, we hear a kind of democratic poetry in the sporty metaphors that make our English language so athletic. These phrases and expressions are vivid emblems of the games that we, as a people, watch and play.

As early as A.D. 1300, *box* included the meaning of "a blow." The sense of "a fight with the fists" appeared in 1567. Some historians believe that the term *boxing* came from the Greeks, the earliest practitioners of the sport, and their comparison of the clenched fist to a box (*pyxis*). In ancient Greece, boxing was more brutal sport than it is today. A match didn't end until; one fighter was unconscious or, in some cases, dead.

Other historians attribute the origin to a priest in Siena, Italy, who was later canonized as St. Bernadine. Early in the thirteenth century, Bernadine is alleged to have taught his male parishioners to fight with their fists rather than deadly weapons, emphasizing special techniques to *box up* (block) an opponent's punches with the hands and arms.

Boxing is a knockout sport whose metaphors pervade our language. Here's a blow-by-blow description: Straight from the shoulder (often a devastating blow in the sport), boxing words and expressions pull no punches in our phrases. When fate has us on the ropes and hits us below the belt with a low blow in a knockdown, drag-out fight, we can take it on the chin, get knocked for a loop, go down for the count, and throw in the towel or sponge. Or we can take the gloves off, throw our hat in the ring, roll with the punches, beat our opponent to the punch with a one-two punch, answer the bell, come out swinging, and be saved by the bell. Please remember that I'm in your corner.

The word *soccer* derives from "association football." In the late nineteenth century, the front and the back of *association* were clipped, the terminal *c* hardened, and the slangy – *er* suffix appended: *soc* + *er* = *soccer*. The nickname *rugger*, from *rugby*, was formed the same way, and *bummer* and *to take a header* show the same suffix.

En garde (*fencing*), sports fans. Let's level the playing field. How many sports can you find hidden in the following passage? It's a slam dunk (*basketball*) and a drop kick (*football*) that you employ many of these expressions in your everyday conversations. Let the game begin!

When the situation is up for grabs because your opponent is getting his hackles up, you must knuckle down, hold the line, call the shots, hit the bulls eye, set the bar high, get the ball rolling, spike the ball, score a hat trick, stick your landing, perform a figure eight, take the bull by the horns with no holds barred, win by a nose, and put the pedal to the metal and the ball in the other guy's court.

Otherwise, you may end up jumping the gun, not up to par, down and out, out in left field, behind the eight ball, barking up the wrong tree, throwing a gutter ball, suffering a wipeout, catching a crab, taking the bait hook, line, and sinker and lock, stock, and barrel, or facing a sticky wicket.

Answers

More than thirty sports are represented:

When the situation is up for grabs (*basketball*) because your opponent is getting his hackles up (*cock fighting*), you must knuckle down (*marbles*), hold the line (*football*), call the shots (*billiards*), hit the bulls eye (*archery, shooting*), set the bar high (*high jump, pole vault*), get the ball rolling (*soccer*), spike the ball (*volleyball*), score a hat trick (*ice hockey*), catch a wave (*surfing*), stick your landing (*gymnastics*), perform a figure eight (*figure skating*), take the bull by the horns (*rodeo*) with no holds barred (*wrestling*), win by a nose (*horse racing*), and put pedal to the metal (*auto racing*) and the ball in the other guy's court (*tennis*).

Otherwise, you may end up jumping the gun (*track*), not up to par (*golf*), down and out (*boxing*), out in left field (*baseball*), behind the eight ball (*pool*), barking up the wrong tree (*coon hunting*), throwing a gutter ball (*bowling*), suffering a wipeout (*skiing, skateboarding, etc.*), getting run through (*fencing*), catching a crab (*crew*), facing a sticky wicket (*cricket*)**,** or taking the bait hook, line, and sinker (*fishing*) and lock, stock, and barrel (*shooting*).

Ball's In Your Court

I live and move and have my being in San Diego, where, more than seventy-five years ago, a petite product of our public tennis courts accomplished the greatest feat by a teenager in the history of sport.

In 1953, Maureen "Little Mo" Connolly, at the age of eighteen, became the first woman to win the Grand Slam of tennis—all four majors in a calendar year—losing but a single set. In her meteoric career, cut short by a tragic horseback riding accident in 1954, San Diego native Mo Connolly captured the last nine Grand Slam tournaments that she entered.

Had not her horse, Colonel Merryboy, been spooked by a speeding concrete truck careering around a curve, who knows what unreachable heights Maureen Connolly might have scaled? She was just nineteen, but she never recovered from the awful leg injuries she suffered in the mishap. Only fifteen years later, she succumbed to cancer.

Standing at five feet, two inches, Maureen acquired the nickname "Little Mo" because her lethal ground strokes called to mind the fire power of the World War II battleship U.S.S. Missouri, nicknamed "Big Mo." Remembering Maureen Connolly, who first stepped onto our municipal courts brandishing a $1.50 racquet, I offer a small glossary of tennis terms:

tennis. Descended from the French *tenez*, "take heed," "mark," "receive." Frequently used to start a match, *tennis* became the name of the game itself.

court. From the Norman French *cort,* "an enclosed area of yard." Court tennis, the forerunner of the modern game, was played mainly in courtyards.

deuce. This scoring term descends from the French *a deux le jeu,* "two to play." At forty-all, one side must win two points in a row to achieve victory.

A *let ball* is a serve that brushes the net but lands fair in the serve box, giving the server another chance to put the ball in play. From Old English *lettan,* "to hinder, delay."

love. Spook etymology, which I spoke about early in this book, has been served up in the game of tennis, where *love* means "no points." The most deceptively charming derivation for the use of *love* in this sense is that the word derives from *l'ouef*—"the egg"—because a zero resembles an egg, just as the Americanism "goose egg" stands for "zero." But *un oeuf,* rather than *l'ouef,* would be the more likely French form, and, anyway, the French themselves designate "no score" in tennis by saying "zero."

Most tennis historians adhere to a less imaginative but more plausible theory. These more level heads contend that the tennis term is rooted in the Old English expression "neither love nor money," which is more than a thousand years old. Because love is the antithesis of money, as in the phrase a *labor of love,* it is nothing.

poach. From Old French *pochier,* "to pocket," which came to mean "to encroach or trespass for game; to steal."

racquet. From the Arabic *rahat,* "palm of the hand." The earliest racquets were palm-shaped bats used by the Persians as early as the fourth century.

round robin. The *robin* in *round* robin descends from the French *ruban,* or "ribbon." During the seventeenth and eighteenth centuries in France, it was a brave man indeed who had the courage to address a grievance to the crown. To avoid losing one's head—literally—some clever complainants devised a *rond ruban,* a method for taking grievances to superiors with the document signed in circular form by the petitioners so that no one name would head the list.

seed. Despite the fact that this word is often erroneously spelled *cede,* what we have here is an agricultural metaphor. In tennis tournaments the highest-ranked players are separated like seeds drawn from a husk and then strewn around the field of entrants.

serve. From the Old French *servir,* "to labor as a servant," attesting to the relative unimportance of the first shot in a point in the early days of tennis. Clearly this term was coined before the careers of Andy Roddick and Venus Williams.

volley. From the Middle French *volée,* "flight," a derivative of the Latin *volare,* "to fly." The application to tennis is first recorded in 1596 for the action of hitting a ball in flight before it has bounced. When you exchange shots with your opponent from the back court, that is a rally, not a volley.

Here's an addendum about pickleball, the fastest-growing sport across our fair land. A quarter-size version of tennis, greatly influenced by badminton, ping-pong, and Wiffle ball, pickleball is all the rage.

The game started during the summer of 1965 on Bainbridge Island, a short ferry ride from Seattle, Washington. Then State Representative Joel Pritchard and two of his friends—Bill Bell and Barney McCallum—returned from golf one Saturday afternoon and found their families bored with the usual summertime activities. They tried to set up badminton, but no one could find the shuttlecock. So they improvised with a Wiffle ball, lowered the badminton net, and fabricated paddles of plywood from a nearby shed.

According to Joan Pritchard, Joel's wife, the name of the sport came "after I said it reminded me of the Pickle Boat in crew, where oarsmen were chosen from the leftovers of other boats. Somehow the idea the name came from our dog Pickles was attached to the naming of the game, but Pickles wasn't on the scene for two more years. The dog was named for the game."

Par For the Course

Mark Twain called it a good walk spoiled, and Oscar Wilde defined it as a man fanning a ball with a stick. More recently, it has been called an adult version of an Easter-egg hunt.

The activity, of course, is golf.

Personally, I don't play the sport for two linguistic reasons: First, the word *golf* is, appropriately, *flog* spelled backward. Second, I have dedicated my life to being above par and don't wish to flog myself trying to be subpar.

Why did the golfer have to buy a new pair of socks? Because he had a hole in one.

Despite what the internet may tell you, the word *golf* is not an acronym for "gentlemen only, ladies forbidden." In truth, *golf* is derived either from the German *kolbe*, which like the Dutch *colf* and French *chole*, means "stick, club," or from the Scottish *gowf,* "to strike."

In Old and Middle English the word for a young girl was *brid,* from which we get *bride.* By a semantic shift known as metathesis, the *i* and the *r* became transposed, and in the late eighteenth century, *bird* resulted. Crossing the ocean in the mid nineteenth century, *bird* became American slang for a person or thing of excellence. In the early 1920s, the popular word attached itself to golf, in the diminutive form of *birdie,* to signify one stroke under par.

The eagle, the king of birds, is often a symbol of excellence. Eagle Scout is the loftiest of Boy Scout ranks, and the eagle is an emblem of high military rank. It is no surprise, then, that a score of two below par in golf is *an eagle*, even better than *a birdie*.

In Great Britain in the early 1890s, a bogey was a ghost or specter. That word gives us both the bogeyman that causes little children to scurry to their beds in fright and the golf term *bogey*, one stroke over par. The operative metaphor here is that the score became like a monstrous opponent, hence, a frightening bogey.

According to legend, Mary, Queen of Scots, was the first female golfer. When she returned to Scotland from France in 1560, several French youths accompanied her to serve as pages and porters. These young men were likened to cadets, "young soldiers," and a golf club porter came to be known as a *caddy*.

Fore, the traditional vocal warning to golfers playing ahead that a ball is about to be struck or is in flight, derives from the Old English preposition that means "in front," as in *forecast, forehead*, and *foreword.*

A *mulligan* is a free shot to compensate for a mishit ball, sometimes permitted in a casual game. No one can say for sure how this word came into golf in 1949, but here's my best guess: In family-type saloons there was always a bottle of a hot sauce called Mulligan on the bar. The basic ingredients of this sauce were hot pepper seeds and water. If you were crazy enough to swish a few drops of this concoction into your beer, it ate out your liver, stomach, bladder, and finally your heart. In the psychological sense, this is precisely what happens on the course when you accumulate too many mulligans.

An alternative theory asserts that the word eponymously derives from the name of Canadian golfer David Mulligan. Each week, Mulligan provided transportation to the St. Lambert Country Club near Montreal for his regular foursome. One day in the late 1920s, he mishit his drive off the first tee with hands still numb from driving over rough roads and a bumpy bridge at the course entrance. In appreciation for Mulligan's driving (of his automobile), his friends gave him a second ball.

A *stymie* was originally a situation in which a player's ball rests between the cup and another ball, obstructing its path. Some suggest that *stymie* issues from the Gaelic *stigh mi,* meaning "inside me," while others point to the Dutch *stuit mij,* meaning "it stops me." Now that players place a marker on the green and remove the impediment, the word has soared off the fairway of golfing parlance and into general use as a verb to mean "to frustrate, thwart, block in reaching a goal."

What's the missing link between golf courses and *links?* The term arrived from the Anglo-Saxon word *hlinc,* meaning "rising ground or ridge" and refers to sandy areas and ridges along a coast. True links golf courses, mostly found in England, Ireland, and Scotland, must sit by the coast and on sandy soil. More than with desert or parkland courses, golf links challenge players to battle the natural elements.

Take Me Out to the Ballgame

How was baseball played throughout the Bible? In the big inning, Eve stole first. Adam balked but stole second. Cain struck out Abel. During the great flood, humanity was rained out. Gideon rattled the pitchers. Saul was put out by David. Absalom and Judas went out swinging. And the prodigal son stole home.

Baseball is one of our oldest sports, originating before the Civil War as a game called rounders. Abraham Lincoln played town ball, a local variant of rounders, and may have been playing that game when, in 1860, the news reached him that he had been elected president.

With more than a century and a half of American history, baseball evokes more nostalgia than any other athletic endeavor. No other sports poem is as beloved as Ernest Lawrence Thayer's "Casey at the Bat," published in 1888; and no other sports song is nearly as famous as "Take Me Out to the Ball Game," first recorded in 1908.

In the early days of the twentieth century, a college professor explained, "To understand America, you must understand baseball." Not only is baseball America's pastime, but the source of the most pervasive athletic metaphors in the American language. Whether or not we're fans, we often speak baseballese away from the baseball diamond.

Take the word *blooper*, which first appeared in American English in the mid 1920s as a baseball term describing a wounded fly ball looped just past the reach of the infielders. Just as bloopers in baseball can make fielders look like bumbling clowns, verbal bloopers can mortify those who make them. Almost at the same time, the verb *to bloop* began to signify the operating of a radio set to cause it or other sets to emit howls and whistles, perhaps an echo of our reactions to physical or verbal howlers. About a decade later, the nouns *bloop* and *blooper* came to signify pratfalls of the body and tongue.

You may well know that a *southpaw* is a slang term for a left-handed person, but do you know why? The answer can be found in our great American pastime. Most early baseball diamonds were laid out with the pitcher's mound to the east of home plate. With the westward orientation of home plate, the batter wouldn't have to battle the afternoon sun in his eyes. As a result, as a right-handed pitcher wound up, he faced north—and a left-handed pitcher south. *South + paw* ("hand") = *southpaw*.

A Baseball Game

Fill in each blank below with a common word or phrase that has its origins in baseball. Don't worry. I know that you'll be *in there pitching*. *You'll step up to plate, swing for the fences,* and *hit a home run.*

Answers appear on the scoreboard at end of the game.

1. We're not making a bit of progress with this project. We can't even get to _____ _____.

2. You are so out of it. You're way out there in _____ _____.

3. Some people are born with a silver spoon in their mouth, while others are born with _____ _____ against them.

4. Right off the _____, let's get to work on this project.

5. I know you can't give me an exact price, but can you give me a _____ figure?

6. These people are really serious. They play _____.

7. On Broadway, the new musical comedy has been a _____ _____.

8. I promise I'll consult you before I make any decisions. I'll be sure to _____ _____ with you.

9. I can't meet with you today, but I'd like to in the near future. May I take a _____ _____?

10. Before we submit the proposal, we need to _____ _____ a few ideas.

11. She's such a wild and wacky woman–a real _____.

12. Throckmorton is away at a conference, so we're going to have Gump _____ _____ for him.

13. Be straight with me. Don't throw me any _____.

14. That business presentation was great. It was a _____ _____ performance.

15. They're inexperienced, and they're incompetent. They run a _____ _____ operation.

Answers

1. first base 2. left field 3. two strikes 4. bat 5. ballpark

6. hardball 7. smash hit 8. touch base 9. rain check 10. bat around

11. screwball 12. pinch-hit 13. curveballs 14. major league 15. bush-league/minor-league

☺A Guide to Sportspeak

The English language and the game of baseball would be immeasurably poorer without the fractured diction and disheveled grammar of St. Louis pitcher and announcer Dizzy Dean. Dean peppered his commentaries with *ain't*s and double negatives, and when he judged a verb too colorless, he invented his own, as in "He slud into third base" and "The pitcher flang the ball."

When an indignant listener complained, "Mr. Dean. Don't you know the King's English?" Dizzy reflected for a moment and replied, "Sure I do—and so's the Queen!"

Ever since Dizzy Dean's verbal vagaries, broadcasters have been striking out, shanking foul balls, and caught stealing home with the English language. Here are some samples of "Colemanisms" from Jerry Coleman, longtime broadcaster for my home team, the San Diego Padres:

- Sunday is Senior Citizens' Day. And if you want to become a senior citizen, just call the Padres ticket office.
- Mike Caldwell, the Padres' right-handed southpaw, will pitch tonight.
- If Pete Rose brings the Reds in first, they ought to bronze him and put him in cement.
- [Dave] Winfield goes back to the wall. He hits his head on the wall, and it rolls off. It's rolling all the way back to second base. This is a terrible thing for the Padres.

- Ozzie Smith just made another play that I've never seen anyone else make before, and I've seen him make it more often than anyone else ever has.

Jerry Coleman is not alone. Here are more bloopers out of other broadcast booths:

- He's already got two championship rings under his belt.
- It appears as though the Achilles' heel of the Eagles' defense is about to rear its ugly head.
- Arnold Palmer, usually a great putter, is having trouble with his long putts. However, he has no trouble dropping his shorts.
- That long drive actually sailed into the second balcony and hit a fan on the fly.
- Folks, this is perfect weather for today's game. Not a breath of fresh air.
- Just don't think that Boston is going blow up and dry away.
- Anytime Boston scores more than a hundred points and holds the other team below a hundred points, they almost always win.
- That's one of the best sets I've ever seen Thomas Zib play—although I should preface that by saying I've never seen him play before.
- Leo Label has been competing with a pulled stomach muscle, showing a lot of guts.
- The seventy-eight-yard drive was led by fourteen-year-old veteran Len Dawson.

Hats In the Ring

A Primer of Political Words

Although the classical societies of ancient Greece and Rome have vanished, Greek and Roman thought is very much alive in the parlance of politics. As the joke goes, the etymology of the word *politics* derives from *poly*, "many," and *tics*, which are blood-sucking parasites. In truth, *politics* issues from the Greek word *polities*, "city, citizen." Politics may make strange bedfellows, but, as we shall see, politics makes for even stranger, and sometimes colorful, vocabulary.

Taking first things first, I'll start with the word *primary*, which descends from the Latin *primus*, "first." *Primary*, as a shortening of "primary election, is first recorded in 1861. In an *election* we "pick out" a candidate whom we wish to vote for. In Latin *e* means "out" and *lectus* "pick or choose."

Campaign is very much a fighting word. The Latin *campus*, "field," is a clue that the first campaigns were conducted on battlefields. A military campaign is a series of operations mounted to achieve a particular wartime objective. A political campaign is an all-out effort to secure the election of a candidate to office.

When he went to the Forum in Roman times, a *candidate* for office wore a bleached white toga to symbolize his humility, purity of motive and candor. The original Latin root, *candidatus*, meant "one who wears white," from the belief that white was the color of purity and probity. There was wishful thinking even in ancient Roman politics, even though a white-clad Roman *candidatus* was accompanied by *sectatores*, followers who helped him get votes by bargaining and bribery. The Latin parent verb *candere*, "to shine, to glow" can be recognized in the English words *candid, candor, candle, chandelier,* and *incandescent.*

We know that candidates are ambitious; it's also worth knowing that *ambition* developed from the Latin *ambitionem,* "a going about," from the going about of candidates for office in ancient Rome.

President descends from the Latin *praesidio,* "preside, sit in front of or protect." Presidents sit in the seat of government. When we speak of "the ship of state," we are being more accurate etymologically than we know. The Greek word *kybernao* meant "to direct a ship." The Romans borrowed the word as *guberno,* and ultimately it crossed the English Channel as *governor,* originally a steersman. That's why the noun is *governor* and the adjective *gubernatorial.*

The story behind the word *inaugurate* is an intriguing one. The word literally means "to take omens from the flight of birds." In ancient Rome, augurs would predict the outcome of an enterprise by the way the birds were flying. "To auger well" means "to prophesy favorably." Augurs (the first "early birders") were also known as auspices, whence our word *auspicious,* from the Latin *avis,* "bird" + *specere,* "to observe."

These soothsayers, magicians, and priests would tell a general whether to march or to do battle by the formations of the birds on the wing. They might even catch one and cut it open to observe its entrails for omens. Nowadays, presidential candidates use their inauguration speeches to take flight on an updraft of words, rather than birds—and they often spill their guts for all to see.

Filibuster is imported from the Dutch *vrijbuiter,* "freebooter," which first meant "pirate, adventurer, one who plunders freely" in English. That sense is retained in the current denotation of *filibuster:* "holding a piece of legislation captive by making long and windy speeches." One of the first known practitioners of the filibuster was the Roman senator Cato the Younger. In debates over legislation he especially opposed, Cato would often obstruct the measure by speaking continuously until nightfall.

The verb *to ostracize* means "to exclude from a group by popular consent," and hidden in that verb is an oyster. Rather than clamming up and floundering, just for the halibut let's go fishing for the origin of *ostracize*. Oysters were a staple of the ancient Greek diet, and the verb *to ostracize* descends directly from *ostrakon*, the Greek word for an oyster shell and also for a broken piece of pottery. In ancient Athens, the people could banish a politician by popular vote. Citizens gathered in the market place and wrote down the name of the undesirable on a tile or potsherd. If enough votes were dropped into an urn, the "winner" was sent from the city for either five or ten years. Because the shards of pottery resembled oyster shells, they were called *ostrakon*, whence our verb for general exclusion.

Centuries after the *ostrakon*, Italians used small balls or pebbles to vote, "casting" them into one box or another. Hence, the word *ballot*, "a small ball or pebble." If a majority of black balls were placed in a ballot box, the candidate was *blackballed*, "excluded, ostracized."

The original Greek meaning of the word *idiot* was not a matter of I.Q. Long before the psychologists got hold of the word, the Greeks used *idiotes*, from the root *idios*, "private," as in *idiom* and *idiosyncrasy*, to designate those who did not hold public office. Because such people possessed no special status or skill, the word *idiot* gradually fell into disrepute.

The *vote* that responsible citizens cast is really a "vow" or "wish." And this is the precise meaning of the Latin *votum*. People in our society who fail to exercise their democratic privilege of voting on election day are sometimes called idiots.

The political expression "to throw one's hat in the ring" probably derives from the custom of tossing one's hat into the boxing ring to signal the acceptance of a pugilist's challenge. Once the hat is thrown, the candidates start engaging in political infighting as they slug it out with their opponents.

During the nineteenth century, a dedicated follower showed support for a political candidate by carrying a torch in an evening campaign parade. A fellow who "carried a torch" in such a rally didn't care who knew that he was wholeheartedly behind his candidate. Later the term was applied to someone publicly (and obsessively) in love.

One more metaphor that was originally literal attaches to bandwagons, high wagons large enough to hold a band of musicians. Early bandwagons were horse-drawn through the streets in order to publicize an upcoming event. Political candidates would ride a bandwagon through a town, and those who wished to show their support would "hop [or climb] on the bandwagon" and ride with the candidate and his blaring band.

Horses and horse racing are dominant animal metaphors that gallop through political life. One of the earliest of equine metaphors is "dark horse." The figure refers to a political candidate who is nominated unexpectedly, usually as a result of compromise between two factions in a party. Dark horse candidates who became president include James Polk in 1844, Franklin Pierce in 1852, Rutherford B. Hayes in 1876, James Garfield in 1880, and Warren G. Harding in 1920.

Presidents always have running mates. This too is a horse racing term and derives from the practice of one owner or one stable running two horses in a race, the slower one being put in there to pace the star. The pacesetter was known as the star's running mate. The phrase has been around for more than a century, but its use to define a vice president was coined by, of all non-practitioners of slang, Woodrow Wilson. At the Democratic Convention in 1912 the presidential nomination went to Wilson on the forty-sixth ballot after a terrific brawl. Governor Wilson of New Jersey announced that his vice-presidential choice would be another governor, Thomas Marshall, and announced, "And I feel honored by having him as my running mate." Wilson's turn of phrase brought the house down, the only squeak of humor those assembled had ever heard out of Woodrow Wilson.

Presidential jockeying for position gets out of the gate earlier and earlier with each campaign. It remains to be seen whether the next presidential contest will turn out to be a runaway or a real horse race. Will a dark horse give the frontrunner a run for his or her money? Will the old war horse and his or her running mate, saddled with international and economic problems, turn out to be shoo-ins or lame ducks?

OK!

Explanations for the origin of *OK* have been as imaginative as they have been various. But Professor Allen Walker Read, a professor at Columbia University, proved that *OK* did not derive from *okeh*, an affirmative reply in Choctaw; nor from the name of chief Old Keokuk; nor from a fellow named Orrin Kendall, who manufactured a tasty brand of army biscuit for Union soldiers in the Civil War; nor from the Haitian port Aux Cayes, which produced superior rum; nor from "open key," a telegraph term; nor from the Greek *olla kalla*, "all good."

Professor Read demonstrated that *OK* started life as an obscure joke and through a twist of fate went to the top of the charts on the American hit parade of words. In the 1830s, in New England, there was a craze for initialisms, in the manner of *FYI*, *LOL*, OMG, and *TGIF*, so popular today. The fad went so far as to generate letter combinations of intentionally comic misspellings: *KG* for "know go," *KY* for "know yuse," *NSMJ* for "'nough said 'mong jentlemen," and *OR* for "oll wrong." *OK* for "oll korrect" naturally followed.

Of all those loopy initialisms and facetious misspellings, *OK* alone survived. That's because of a presidential nickname that consolidated the letters in the national memory. Martin Van Buren, elected our eighth president in 1836, was born in Kinderhook, New York, and, early in his political career, was dubbed "Old Kinderhook." Echoing the "Oll Korrect" initialism, *OK* became the rallying cry of the Old Kinderhook Club, a Democratic organization supporting Van Buren during the 1840 campaign. Thus, the

OK!

accident of Van Buren's birthplace rescued *OK* from the dustbin of history.

The coinage did Van Buren no good. He was defeated in his bid for re-election. But the word honoring the name of his birthplace today remains what H. L. Mencken identified as "the most shining and successful Americanism ever invented."

Teddy's Bear

Mothers sewed stuffed bears before President Theodore Roosevelt came along, but no one called them teddy bears. Not until November 1902, when Roosevelt traveled to Smedes, Mississippi, where he was acting as adjudicator for a border dispute between Louisiana and Mississippi.

On November 14, during a break in the negotiations, Roosevelt was invited by southern friends to go bear hunting. He felt that he could consolidate his support in the South by appearing there in the relaxed atmosphere of a hunting party, so he accepted the invitation.

During the hunt, Roosevelt's hosts cornered a bear cub, and a guide roped it to a tree for the president to kill. Roosevelt declined to shoot the cub, believing such an act to be beneath his dignity as a hunter and as a man: "If I shot that little fellow, I wouldn't be able to look my boys in the face again."

That Sunday's *Washington Post* carried a cartoon, drawn by artist Clifford Berryman. T.R. stood in hunting gear, rifle in hand and his back toward the cowering cub. The caption read, "Drawing the line in Mississippi," referring both to the border dispute and to animal ethics.

Now the story switches to the wilds of Brooklyn, N.Y. There Russian immigrants Morris and Rose Michtom owned a candy store where they sold refreshments, novelties, and toys, including handmade stuffed animals. Inspired by Berryman's cartoon, Rose Michtom made a toy bear and displayed it in the shop window. The bear proved popular with the public.

The Michtoms sent President Roosevelt the very bear they had put in their window. They said it was meant for Roosevelt's grandchildren and asked T.R. for permission to name the bear after him. The president replied, "I don't know what my name may mean to the bear business, but you're welcome to use it."

Well, T.R.'s name turned out to do a lot for the bear business. Rose and Morris began turning out stuffed cubs labeled *Teddy's bear*, in honor of our twenty-sixth president, and business boomed. As the demand increased, the family hired extra seamstresses and rented a warehouse. Their operation eventually became the Ideal Toy Corporation.

The bear was a prominent emblem in Roosevelt's successful 1904 election campaign, and *Teddy's bear* was enshrined in dictionaries in 1907. Cartoonist Berryman never sought compensation for the use of the cub he had created. He simply smiled and said, "I have made thousands of children happy. That is enough for me."

☺Political Tickles

More than 2,500 years ago, the fabulist Aesop observed, "We hang the petty thieves and appoint the great ones to public office." Ambrose Bierce sardonically defined *politics* as "A strife of interest masquerading as a contest of principles." Robert Louis Stevenson noted that "politics is perhaps the only profession for which no preparation is thought necessary." President Ronald Reagan quipped, "Politics is supposed to be the second oldest profession. I have come to realize that it bears a very close resemblance to the first." H. L. Mencken defined a politician as "a man who will double-cross that bridge when he comes to it."

That's the same H. L. Mencken who observed, "Under democracy, one party always devotes its chief energies to trying to prove that the other party is unfit to rule—and both commonly succeed, and are right." Mencken's contemporary, Clarence Darrow, echoed that sentiment: "When I was a boy I was told that anybody could become President. Now I'm beginning to believe it."

In support of Darrow's point, remember that Jefferson did it, Nixon did it, and Truman did it. So any Tom, Dick, and Harry can become President of the United States!

Have you ever wondered: If *pro* and *con* are opposites, is congress the opposite of progress? Mark Twain loved to pick on members of Congress: "No man's life, liberty, or property are safe while the legislature is in session," he declared, as well as "Talk is cheap, except when Congress does it" and "It could probably be shown by facts and figures that there is no distinctly native American criminal class, except Congress." His sharpest congressional barbs go like this: "First God made idiots for practice, and then He made congressmen." and "Suppose you were an idiot. And suppose you were a member of Congress. But I repeat myself."

Politicians have been riddled by riddles:

- What do we call voting in America? *Electile Dysfunction.*
- How can you tell when a politician is lying? *His lips are moving.*
- Have you heard about the new dance called The Politician? *You take three steps forward, two steps backward, then side-step, side-step, and reverse direction.*
- What do politicians and diapers have in common? *They both need changing regularly—and for the same reason.*
- Why should all politicians wear uniforms, like NASCAR drivers? *So that we can identify their corporate sponsors.*

Political jokes can be very powerful. That's why so many of them get elected. Will Rogers explained, "I don't make jokes. I just watch the government and report the facts." Jay Leno observed, "If God wanted us to vote, he would have given us candidates." On the campaign trail, Adlai Stevenson confessed, "I offered my opponents a deal: If they stop telling lies about me, I will stop telling the truth about them." And Charles de Gaulle summed it all up this way: "I have come to the conclusion that politics is too serious a matter to be left to the politicians."

That's why *political science* is an oxymoron.

☺AMERICAN HISTORY ACCORDING TO STUDENT BLOOPERS

It is truly astounding what havoc students can wreak upon the chronicles of the human race. I have pasted together a chronicle of U.S. "history" from student bloopers collected by teachers throughout the world, from eighth grade through college level.

Read carefully, and you will learn a lot.

Christopher Columbus was a great nagivator who discovered America while cursing about the Atlantic Ocean on the Nina, the Pinta Colada, and the Santa Fe.

Later, Jamestown was discovered by King James the One and named after him. The Pilgrims drove the Mayflower across the ocean and arrived in hardships. This was called the Pill's Grim Progress. These people always wore old shoes with a big buckle on the top of them. The men wore pants that only came a little way past their knees, and the girls wore funny bonnets.

The winter of 1620 was a hard one for the settlers. Many people died, and many babies were born. Captain John Smith was responsible for all this.

One of the causes of the Revolutionary War was the English put tacks in their tea. The Boston Tea Party was a raid where they threw all the tea into Boston Harbor, which they all drank. Finally, General Corn Wallace surrendered and the War was over. When General Burgundy surrendered to Sara's Toga, the colonists won the war and no longer had to pay for taxis.

American History According to Student Bloopers

America was founded by four fathers. Delegates from the original thirteen states formed the Contented Congress. Thomas Jefferson, a Virgin, and Benjamin Franklin were two singers of the Decoration of Independence, which says that all men are cremated equal and are well endowed by their creator.

Benjamin Franklin had gone to Boston carrying all his clothes in his pocket and a loaf of bread under each arm. He invented electricity by rubbing two cats backwards and declared, "A horse divided against itself cannot stand." Franklin died in 1790 and is still dead.

George Washington crossed the Delaware River, married Martha Custis, and in due time became the Father of Our Country. The difference between a king and a president is that a king is the son of his father, but a president isn't. Washington's farewell address was Mount Vernon.

Soon the Constitution of the United States was adopted to secure domestic hostility. Under the Constitution, the people have the right to bare arms.

In the early nineteenth century, Lois and Clark explored the Louisiana Purchase. The two greatest marshals of the Old West were Wyatt Burp and Wild Bill Hiccup. General George Custard extinguished himself at the Battle of the Little Big Horn.

Abraham Lincoln became America's greatest Precedent. Lincoln's mother died in infancy, and he was born in a log cabin which he built with his very own hands. When Lincoln was president, he wore only a tall silk hat. He said, "In onion there is strength." Lincoln wrote the Emasculation Proclamation, and he kept our country in one peace. His last residence was at the Gettysburg Address. Lincoln wrote the Gettysburg Address while traveling from Washington to Gettysburg on the back of an envelope.

On the night of April 14, 1865, Lincoln went to the theater and got shot in his seat by one of the actors in a moving picture show. The believed assinator was John Wilkes Booth, a supposingly insane actor. This ruined Booth's career.

During the Industrial Revolution, people stopped reproducing by hand and started reproducing by machine. The invention of the steamboat by Robert Fulton caused a network of rivers to spring up. Samuel Morse invented a code of telepathy. Eli Whitney invented the spinning gin. Thomas Edison invented the pornograph and the indecent lamp. Andrew Carnegie started the steal business. And George Goethals dug the alimentary canal.

The First World War was caused by the assignation of the Arch-Duck by an anahist.

Charles Limburger was the first man to ever cross the Atlantic alone. He wanted to go by regular airlines, but he couldn't afford to buy a ticket. When he got to Paris, all the French people shouted, "Bonsai!"

World War II happened when Adolph Hitler and the Knotsies had erotic dreams of conquest all over Europe. Wilt Chamberlain practiced appeasement in Europe before the Second World War. Franklin Roosevelt put a stop to Hitler, who committed suicide in his bunk.

Martin Luther had a dream. He went to Washington and recited his Sermon on the Monument. Later, he nailed ninety-six Protestants in the Watergate Scandal, which ushered in a new error in the anals of human history.

The Annals of Science

Brave New Words

It wasn't that long ago that, in the course of a typical lifetime, only the cast of characters playing out the human drama changed, not the drama itself. But starting with the Industrial Revolution in eighteenth-century England and nineteenth-century America, the text of the play itself began changing, and these days it seems to be revised daily. The world spins faster, and the speed of technical advance can make us dizzy.

Hail and farewell to rumble seats and running boards. Iceboxes and Frigidaires. Victrolas and hi-fi's. Fountain pens and inkwells. Telephone booths and party lines. Test patterns. Tennis presses. Slide rules. Manual typewriters. Corrasable Bond, photostats, and mimeographs.

The inexorable advance of technology shapes our culture and the language that reflects it. We used to watch the tube, but televisions aren't made of tubes anymore, so that figure of speech has disappeared. Something that irritated us was like fingernails scraping across a blackboard, but nowadays it's all whiteboards, and they don't squeak.

We used to dial telephone numbers and dial up people and places. Then came pushbutton phones and then cell phones, so we scramble for a new verb—"Sorry, I must have pushed the wrong number"; "I think I'll punch up Doris"; "I've got to tap the Internal Revenue Service"; *Press M for Murder*—and watch *dial* dying on the vine.

How many more years do *hot off the press, hung out to dry, put through the wringer,* and *carbon copy* have, now that we no longer print with hot lead, hang wet clothes on clotheslines, operate wringer washing machines, and copy with carbon? Despite the electrifying rise of online reading, I tightly cross my fingers that we won't have to bid farewell to the *paper* in *newspaper*.

Do any young folks still say, "This is where we came in?" The statement means the action or situation is starting to repeat itself, and it comes from the movies. Today there are so many ways of finding out exactly when a movie begins, but back in the day, we'd get to the theater at pretty much any time and walk in at random. We might watch the last half of a movie and then some trailers, a newsreel and cartoons (which the multiplexes don't show anymore) and then the second movie in the double feature and then the beginning of the first movie until the point where we could say, "This is where we came in."

Do I sound like a broken record? Do you think I must have been vaccinated with a phonograph needle? In our high-tech times, these metaphors fade away, like photographs left out in the sun.

Remember when *IBM* was something a two-year-old might say to a parent? The computer, the most deeply striking technology of our lifetimes, has powerfully challenged our sense of so many hitherto uncomplicated words: *application, back up, bit, boot, click, cloud, cookie, crash, hacker, icon, mail, memory, menu, mouse, pop-up, program, scroll, spam, surf, virus, window, worm, zip,* and *zoom.*

Then there's the expression *all thumbs*, which used to mean "clumsy with one's hands," as in "Whenever I have to give the baby a bath, I'm all thumbs." Nowadays one who texts speedily and accurately on a Smart Phone is "all thumbs," and that's a compliment.

As science shrinks our world, the language of distance changes. Remember that admonition "Shhh. I'm on long distance!"? Phrases like *long distance, coast-to-coast,* and even *worldwide* used to hold such excitement for us. Now we take them for granted, so we hardly ever use them.

Just as one never steps into the same river twice, one cannot step into the same language twice. Even as one enters, words are swept downstream into the past, forever making a different river. We at the far end of the chronological and language arc have the advantage of remembering that there are words that once did not exist and that there were words that once strutted their hour upon the stage and now are heard no more, except in our collective memory. We also recognize that there are words, many of them technical, that have donned dramatically new meanings. It's one of the great advantages of aging. We can have archaic and eat it too.

Immortal Mortals

In the early nineteenth, British engineer John L. McAdam invented a durable material for repairing roads. We use a form of his name for both the material, *macadam,* and the act of applying it, *macadamize.*

The surest way to grab yourself a place in the English language is to invent a gadget or product so original and useful that people will have to call it by your name, often lowercased. Here are the names of fifteen clever inventors who have done just that. Briefly identify what each of the men below invented:

1. Jim Bowie
2. Robert Wilhelm Bunsen
3. Louis Daguerre
4. Henry Derringer
5. Rudolph Diesel
6. Richard Gatling
7. Johannes Wilhelm Geiger
8. Joseph Hansom
9. Charles McIntosh
10. John Mason
11. George Pullman
12. Henry Shrapnel
13. John Philip Sousa
14. Oliver Winchester
15. Ferdinand, Count von Zeppelin

IMMORTAL MORTALS

Answers

1. Bowie knife 2. Bunsen burner 3. daguerreotype (photographic process) 4. derringer pistol 5. diesel engine
6. Gatling gun 7. Geiger counter 8. Hansom carriage 9. Mackintosh raincoat 10. Mason jar
11. Pullman railroad car 12. shrapnel (shell fragments) 13. sousaphone 14. Winchester rifle 15. zeppelin airship

In a previous chapter titled "What's My Line," you have seen how people get their names from words already in our language. Now let's consider how the kinship works in both directions, how common words are forged from proper names. These words lose their reference to specific persons and become generic terms in our dictionaries, and when they do, they usually shed their capital letters. Such additions to our vocabulary help our language to remain alive and growing, muscular and energetic.

In ancient times, the gods snatched up the souls of those mortals who had found favor in their eyes and made them into stars so that they could forever shine in the heavens for humankind to see. Some men and women have likewise been endowed with a measure of immortality by having their names transmuted into everyday words because of a discovery, object, deed, or attribute of character associated with them.

The Greeks had a word for people who live on in our everyday conversations—*eponymos*, from which we derive the word *eponym*, meaning "after or upon a name." Thousands of eponyms teem our tongues and dot our dictionaries. Stories of the origins of words made from real or imaginary people are among the richest and most entertaining in our language:

In pre-revolutionary France there lived one Etienne de Silhouette, a controller-general for Louis XV. Because of his fanatical zeal for raising taxes and slashing expenses and pensions, he enraged royalty and citizens alike, who ran him out of office within eight months.

At about the same time that the penny-pinching Silhouette was sacked for his infuriating parsimony, the method of making cutouts of profile portraits by throwing the shadow of the subject on the screen captured the fancy of the Paris public. Because the process was cheap and one that cut back to absolute essentials (a scissors and maybe a knife), the man and the method, in the spirit of ridicule, became associated. Ever since, we have called shadow profiles *silhouettes*, with a lowercase *s*.

In 1812, Elbridge Gerry, governor of Massachusetts, became the inspiration for a political term in our English language. In an effort to sustain his party's power, Gerry divided his state into electoral districts with more regard to politics than to geographical reality.

To a drawing of one of the governor's manipulated districts Gilbert Stuart—the same fellow who had painted the famous portrait of George Washington—added a head, eyes, wings, and claws. According to one version of the story, Stuart exclaimed about his creation, "That looks like a salamander!"

"No," countered the editor of the newspaper in which the cartoon was to appear, "Better call it a *gerrymander!*"

The verb *gerrymander* lives on today to describe the shaping of electoral entities for political gain.

Listen now to the stories of fifteen more immortal mortals:

maverick. Samuel Augustus Maverick, a San Antonio rancher, acquired vast tracts of land and dabbled in cattle raising. When he neglected to brand the calves born into his herd, his neighbors began calling the unmarked calves by his name. Through a process that linguists call generalization, this word has come to designate "one who doesn't follow the common herd."

bloomers. Amelia Jenks Bloomer was an American feminist who helped to publicize the fashionable puffy ladies' drawers that seemed to bloom like linen flowers.

boycott. Charles Cunningham Boycott, an Irish land agent, so enraged his tenants with his rent-collection policies that they threatened his life and property and burnt his figure in effigy. Hence, from Ireland comes the verb that means "to coerce an opponent through ostracism."

mesmerize. Franz Anton Mesmer, a Viennese physician who became the sensation of late-eighteenth-century Europe, treated his patients by fixing them with a piercing gaze, questioning them about their ailments, and stroking them with a wand. Today, a form of his name means "to hypnotize, to fascinate."

spoonerism. The Rev. William Archibald Spooner, head of New College, Oxford, set out to become a birdwatcher but instead became a word-botcher. He became renowned for his hilarious reversals of initial consonants and consonant blends, such as "Three cheers for our queer old dean!"

chauvinist. Nicholas Chauvin, a veteran soldier in the French First Republic and Empire, was ridiculed by his comrades for his excessive devotion to the defeated Napoleon. First used as a synonym for knee-jerk patriotism, his name was picked up during the 1970s by the feminist movement to signify attitudes of male supremacy.

sideburns. A century before Elvis Presley, the handsome face of Civil War general Ambrose E. Burnside was adorned by luxuriant side-whiskers sweeping down from his ears to his clean-shaven chin. As the memory of General Burnside faded, and *burnsides* became meaningless, popular usage interpreted the *sides* half to mean "the sides of the face," in which case *sideburns* made more sense. By 1887, the linguistic flip-flop was complete: *Sideburns* took over.

Melba toast and *peach Melba* (a rare double play). Dame Nellie Melba, a famous Australian coloratura soprano, became so much the toast of the town that a toast was named after her, as well as a peachy dessert.

Pompadour. The Marquise de Pompadour, mistress of King Louis XV, wore her hair swept straight up from the forehead in a style that became the rage of the women of Paris.

ritzy. The European hotels of Swiss magnate Cesar Ritz were so swanky that his surname is now eponymously synonymous with high-class lodgings.

leotard. A snugly fitting body garment worn by dancers and acrobats descends from the name of Jules Leotard, a widely acclaimed French trapeze artist who was the first to perfect the aerial somersault.

maudlin. In the New Testament, Mary Magdalen devotedly followed Jesus and ministered to his needs. Portraits of her by Giotto, Titian, Veronese, and many other artists unfailingly depict her as weeping. From her name we derive an adjective that means "tearfully sentimental."

bowdlerize. Dr. Thomas Bowdler of London was a self-appointed literary censor who published a diluted version of Shakespeare, an edition in which "those words are omitted which cannot with propriety be read aloud to a family." A form of his name has become synonymous with expurgating a book so as not to offend delicate sensibilities.

galvanize. Luigi Galvani was an Italian physiologist who stimulated sudden movement in frogs' legs by touching them with static electricity. Today a form of his name means "to stimulate into action, as if with an electrical charge."

dunce. The sixteenth-century followers of the philosopher John Duns Scotus were sneered at because they clung to their old beliefs instead of accepting the "new learning." Even though Duns Scotus was one of the most brilliant thinkers of the later Middle Ages, we use a variation of his middle name to label people we think are stupid.

😃 Science Fantasies

A fourth-grade teacher gathered her pupils in the Science Corner to review the five senses—sight, hearing, touch, taste, and smell.

"You forgot one of the senses," said one of her charges.

"Which one is that?"

And the child explained, "The sense of humor."

That sixth sense—the sense of humor—pervades the world of science:

- Why can't you trust atoms? They make up everything!
- A proton walks into a bar and asks the bartender for a Coca-Cola. "Are you sure you want a Coke and not a beer?" asks the bartender. The proton replies, "Yes, I'm positive."
- A neutron walks into the same bar and asks how much for a drink. The bartender replies, "For you, no charge."
- What is the first thing you need to split an atom? *A fission license.*
- Have you heard about the nuclear scientist who swallowed some uranium? *She got atomic ache.*
- Have you heard about the nuclear scientist who had too many ions in the fire?
- What sound does a subatomic duck make? *"Quark!"*
- The Higgs Boson walks into a Catholic church. The priest asks, "What are you doing here?" Higgs Boson replies, "You can't have mass without me."

- I recently read a book about anti-gravity and helium. I couldn't put it down.
- A man walks into a library and asks the librarian if there was a book on the shelf about Pavlov's dogs and Schrödinger's cat. The librarian answers, "The title rings a bell, but I'm not sure it's there."
- Nature abhors a vacuum. So does my dog.
- What is HIJKLMNO? *Water (h to o).*
- For chemists, alcohol is not a problem. It's a solution.
- Have you heard about the sick chemists? *If you can't helium and you can't curium, you'll probably have to barium.*
- When Oxygen and Magnesium started dating, I was like O MG!
- What do physicists enjoy doing at sporting events? *The wave.*
- What did the physicist say to the highway patrolman when he stopped her for speeding? *"Actually, officer, if you factor in the earth's rotation, we are all speeding."*
- What's the difference between an introverted engineer and an extroverted engineer? *When the introverted engineer speaks to you, he looks down at his shoes. When the extroverted engineer speaks to you, he looks down at your shoes.*
- The optimist sees the glass as half full. The pessimist sees the glass as half empty. The engineer sees the glass as twice as large as it needs to be.
- A few puns make me numb, but math puns make me number.
- What do you get if you divide the circumference of a jack-o-lantern by its diameter? *Pumpkin pi.*
- Have you heard about the math teacher who went on a diet? *First, she gave up pi. When that didn't work, she decided to try no meals.*
- I'd tell you a joke about infinity, but it doesn't have an ending.
- There's a fine line between a numerator and a denominator. Only a fraction of people will understand this joke.
- If you feel cold, go stand in a corner. It's 90 degrees there.
- Black holes suck.

Science Fantasies

- NASA has built a new restaurant on the moon. The food is great, but the place doesn't have any atmosphere.
- Two antennas got married. The wedding was just so-so, but the reception was excellent.
- An infectious disease walks into a bar. The bartender explains, "We don't serve your kind here." The disease responds, "Well, you're not a very good host."
- Where does bad light end up? *In prism.*

- The most renowned scientists of all time were invited to be honored at the White House. Pierre and Marie Curie radiated enthusiasm. Boyle said he was under too much pressure. Franklin told the hosts to go fly a kite. Heisenberg was uncertain if he could make it. Hawking said he'd try to string enough time together to make a space in his schedule. Archimedes was buoyant about the opportunity. Sagan had billions and billions of other things to do. Pavlov drooled at the thought. Watson and Crick accepted, on the condition that the dance band played the twist. Descartes said he thought not—and disappeared. Da Vinci expressed his regrets for not being able to fly in, but wished that he could. Schrodinger had to take his cat to the vet, or did he?

Classical Words

LATINA NON MORTUA EST

In the so-called good old days in the United States, as in Europe, which supplied the model, anyone who went to secondary school and college studied Latin as a matter of course. Even in the first years of the twentieth century, fully half of high-school students were still taking Latin. Many of those young scholars used to repeat this little jingle:

> Latin is a language
> As dead as it can be.
> First it killed the Romans,
> And now it's killing me!

The days of nearly universal Latin study are gone, and relatively few students are being killed by Latin anymore. But that doesn't mean that Latin has expired, another victim of progress and relevance in a high-tech world.

Although no one speaks Latin as a mother tongue, countless people in many countries still read the language. Although the natural growth of Latin has ended and babies no longer learn it as a first language, the so-called dead language lives in our speech, our writing, and our very thoughts. In fact, the DNA of more than half of our English words is marked by Latin, or Greek-through-Latin, etymons, "meaning-bearing elements."

The word *amateur* is derived from the very first verb that all students of Latin learn—*amo*: "I love." Amateurs do it for the love of it. Whether it be golf, fishing, quilting, or model trains, it can only be out of love that the amateur pours so many hours into an unremunerative pursuit.

Plagiarism, literary thievery, involves the stealing of another's words and ideas. The word retains much of the meaning of the original Latin *plagiarius,* "a kidnapper." A plagiarist is indeed one who has kidnapped the brainchild of another writer. That's why your English teacher told you that plagiarism was serious business.

You may have wondered why we use the abbreviation *lbs.* for *pounds.* Wonder no more. A pound designated a weight, from the Latin *pendere,* "to hang or weigh." The full Latin expression was *libra pondo,* literally "a pound in weight." Over the centuries, *pondo,* "in weight," acquired the meaning of "pound," and *libra* was lost, except in *lb.* That's also why the British pound sterling is designated by £.

Language is derived from *lingua,* the Latin word for *tongue,* reminding us that all aspects of language originate with the spoken code. Language is very old, while writing is relatively new. Humans have been speaking for a half million to a million years, but we have known how to write for less than six thousand years, since the invention of cuneiform writing in Mesopotamia and hieroglyphic writing in ancient Egypt. The written language is simply a reflection of the spoken language, an attempt to represent speech graphically.

Latin was an international language of diplomacy, science, medicine, law, and literature until the end of the sixteenth century. Latin's influence on our language has never died. A good half of the Latin vocabulary has found its way into English, and at least sixty percent of our English words are derived from Latin and Greek through Latin. Battalions of English words from Latin words have marched unchanged for more than two thousand years. Examples of such pristine words include *actor, agenda, alibi, animal, basis, benefactor, camera, campus, character, circus, comma, crisis. deficit, diploma, doctor, drama, echo, editor, elevator, epitome, ergo, extra, favor, focus, formula, genius, gusto, honor, humor, hyphen, interest, interior, item, janitor, labor, liquor, major, maximum, medium, minus, motor, narrator, nausea, neuter, oasis, omen, opera, paralysis, plus, prior, professor, quota, rancor, recipe, rigor, rumor, saliva, sculptor, senator, senior, series, splendor, terror, trio, trivia, ulterior, vacuum,* and *veto.*

If Latin derivatives were suddenly stricken from our vocabulary, we would be tongue-tied. Because Latin word parts are so ubiquitous (from the Latin *ubique,* "everywhere"), it is important to learn something about them. As one editor puts it, "Latin improves our ability to read, write, and speak our own tongue."

The Preamble to the U.S. Constitution, for example, wouldn't make sense without the words I've italicized, which are all derived from Latin: "We the *people* of the *United States, in order* to *form* a more *perfect Union,* establish *justice,* insure *domestic tranquility, provide* for the *common defense, promote* the *general* welfare, and *secure* the blessings of *liberty* to ourselves and our *posterity,* do *ordain* and *establish* this *Constitution* for the *United States* of *America.*"

Note the word *preamble.* Every first-year Latin student learns that the verb *ambulare* means "to walk" and that the common prefix *pre* – (as in *prefix*) derives from a Latin preposition meaning "in front of, before." Thus, the student of Latin knows that a preamble is something that comes walking before something else. In the case of the Constitution, the Preamble is a short, important, philosophic statement that walks before the actual Articles of Constitution.

Every time you open your wallet and pull out a dollar bill, you are exposed to Latin. *E pluribus unum* means "one out of many." As the motto of the United States, it refers to one government formed from many states, races, religions, ethnicities, creeds, and national origins.

The eight grammatical categories of English words are all renditions of Latin terms— *noun, pronoun, verb, adjective, adverb, preposition, conjunction,* and *interjection.*

Latin is deeply woven into the language of science. The word *science* itself derives from the Latin *scientia,* "knowledge," and the periodic table is filled with Latin names for elements, including aluminum, cesium, and platinum. Latin is the international language of botany and zoology. More than two hundred and fifty thousand species of flowering plants have Latin or Latinized names.

In astronomy, six of the eight planets in our solar system—Mercury, Venus, Mars, Jupiter, Saturn, Neptune, and the demoted Pluto—are named for Roman gods.

A high percentage of medical terms are Latin, including *Rx*, a Latin symbol for *recipe*. Law employs a lot of Latin terms, such as *ad hominem, habeas corpus, nolo contendere, quid pro quo, non compos mentis, caveat emptor, in extremis, in flagrante delicto, in loco parentis,* and *ipso facto*. Every rank in the U.S. Army from private to general is of Latin origin; and, although abandoned as its liturgical language, Latin is still the official language of the Roman Catholic Church.

The motto for the Olympic games is *"citius, altius, fortius,"* three Latin words that translate to "faster, higher, stronger."

Latin is alive and well and living robustly in the phrases that we use every day. To demonstrate how a knowledge of Latin gives one an *ad*-vantage, I could *ad lib* ("at will, to improvise") *ad infinitum* ("to infinity, endlessly") and *ad nauseam* ("to the point of sickness or disgust"). Instead, I offer, alphabetically, a short list of *bona fide* ("in good faith, genuine") Latin phrases that are commonly used and encountered by speakers of English, along with translations:

alma mater: "nurturing mother," usually with reference to schools and colleges; *alter ego:* "one's second self"; *anno Domini:* "in the year of our Lord"; *ante bellum:* "before the war," especially applied to the period before the American Civil War; *a priori:* "from the former," deductive reasoning from causes to effects, the opposite of *a posteriori: "from the last"*;

carpe diem: "seize the day"; caveat emptor: "Let the buyer beware"; *cum laude:* "with praise, with academic honors"; *de facto:* "existing by fact," opposite of *de jure,* "existing by law"; *delirium tremens:* "delusions and trembling"; *dramatis personae:* "characters in a play"; *et al.:* shortening of *et alia*: "and others"; *et cetera:* "and the rest";

Homo sapiens: "human beings as a thinking species"; *in absentia:* "in the absence of"; *in memoriam:* "in memory of"; *in re:* "in the matter of"; *magnum opus:* "most important work"; *mea culpa:* "I am guilty" (These days the more fashionable iteration is *my bad*); *modus operandi:* "method of operation"; *non compos mentis:* "not in control of one's mind"; *non sequitur:* "it does not follow"; *nota bene:* "note well";

per annum: "each year"; *per capita:* "by head"; *per diem:* "each day"; *per se:* "by itself"; *persona non grata:* "unwelcome person"; *post facto:* "after the fact"; *prima facie:* "at first impression"; *quid pro quo:* "this for that, something for something";

reductio ad absurdum: "reduction to the absurd"; *rigor mortis:* "stiffness of death"; *RIP:* abbreviation of *requiescat in pace,* "rest in peace"; *sine qua non:* "that without which, essential precondition"; *status quo:* "things as they are"; *tempus fugit:* "time flies."

Another compelling reason for learning Latin is to read one of the great literatures of the world in its own tongue. Readers become acquainted with the Roman Empire and its people through its most articulate leaders and thinkers, thus gaining a perspective on their own social and political world. For six hundred years Roman history was world history. Roman civilization, more than any other, formed our own. Nothing more succinctly expresses the need to take a backward glance o'er traveled roads through the classics than the Afro-American saying "If somebody asks where you goin', tell 'em where you been."

Nota Bene: Latina non mortua est: Latin is not dead.

Dig Down to the Roots

Words and people have a lot in common. Like people, words are born, grow up, get married, have children, and even die. And, like people, words come in families—big and beautiful families. A word family is a cluster of words that are related because they contain the same root; a root is a basic building block of language from which a variety of related words are formed. You can expand your vocabulary by digging down to the roots of an unfamiliar word and identifying the meanings of those roots.

For example, knowing that the roots *scribe* and *script* mean "write" will help you to deduce the meanings of a prolific clan of words, including *ascribe, conscript, describe, inscribe, manuscript, nondescript, postscript, prescribe, proscribe, scribble, scripture,* and *transcribe.* For another example, once you know that *dic* and *dict* are roots that mean "speak or say," you possess a key that unlocks the meanings of dozens of related words, including *abdicate, benediction, contradict, dedicate, dictator, Dictaphone, diction, dictionary, dictum, edict, indicate, indict, interdict, jurisdiction. malediction, predict, syndicate, valedictorian, verdict, vindicate,* and *vindictive.*

Suppose that you encounter the word *antipathy* in speech or writing. From words like *antiwar* and *antifreeze* you can infer that the root *anti –* means "against," and from words like *sympathy* and *apathy* that *path* is a root that means "feeling." From such insights it is but a short leap to deduce that *antipathy* means "feeling against something." This process of rooting out illustrates the old saying "It's hard by the yard but a cinch by the inch."

Dig Down to the Roots

Earlier in this Pleasury I trotted out the word *desultory*, a member of the *sult* family meaning "jump or leap." *Insult* first meant "to attack suddenly, assault," from the Latin *in-*, "upon," and *salio*, "to leap, jump." When you *insult* people, you figuratively jump on them. When you *exult*, you jump for joy. Other members of the *sult* family appear as *sal*, *sil*, and *sault*. *Salient* facts are those that leap out to your attention. *Resilient* people jump back to their original state after suffering an *assault*. To execute a *somersault* is to leap while swinging your heels above (*somer*, from *supra*, "above") your head.

You can expand your verbal powers by learning to look an unfamiliar word squarely in the eye and asking, "What are the roots in the word, and what do they mean?" Here are twenty classical word parts descended from either Latin or Greek, each followed by three words containing each root. From the meanings of the clue words, deduce the meaning of each root, as in PHON – microphone, phonics, telephone = *sound*.

1. AUTO – autobiography, autograph, automaton = _____
2. CHRON – chronic, chronology, synchronize = _____
3. CULP – culpable, culprit, exculpate = _____
4. EU – eugenics, eulogy, euphemism = _____
5. GREG – congregation, gregarious, segregate = _____

6. LOQU – eloquent, loquacious, soliloquy = _____
7. MAGN – magnanimous, magnify, magnitude = _____
8. NOV – innovation, novelty, renovate = _____
9. OMNI – omnipotent, omniscient, omnivorous = _____
10. PHIL – bibliophile, philanthropy, philology = _____

11. SOL – isolate, soliloquy, solitary = _____
12. SOPH – philosopher, sophistication, sophomore = _____
13. TELE – telegraph, telephone, television = _____
14. TEN – tenacious, tenure, untenable = _____
15. TRACT – extract, intractable, tractor = _____

16. VAC – evacuate, vacation, vacuum = _____
17. VERT – convert, introvert, vertigo = _____
18. VIV – survivor, vivacious, vivid = _____
19. VOC – invoke, vocal, vociferous = _____
20. VOL – malevolent, volition, voluntary = _____

Answers

1. self 2. time 3. blame 4. good 5. kind, species
6. speak 7. large 8. new 9. all 10. love
11. alone 12. wise, wisdom 13. far away 14. hold 15. pull
16. empty 17. turn 18. life, lively 19. call, voice 20. wish

A spectacular example of digging down to the classical roots is the thirty-four-letter *supercalifragilisticexpialidocious,* invented for the film version of *Mary Poppins* (1964), which has become our best-known really, really big word.

Etymologically, this is not entirely a nonsense word: *super:* "above" + *cali:*"beauty" + *fragilistic:* "delicate" + *expiali:* "to atone" + *docious:* "educable." Stitched together, *supercalifragilisticexpialidocious* means "atoning for extreme and delicate beauty [while being] highly educable."

The word has also inspired what I believe to be the most bedazzling syllable-by-syllable set-up pun ever devised:

One of the greatest men of the twentieth century was the political leader and ascetic Mahatma Gandhi. His denial of the earthly pleasures included the fact that he never wore anything on his feet. He walked barefoot everywhere. Moreover, he ate so little that he developed delicate health and nauseatingly bad breath. Thus, he became known as a *super callused fragile mystic hexed by halitosis!*

A God is Hiding in Your Sentence

Of all the literary sources that feed into our English language, mythology is one of the richest. The ancient gods, goddesses, heroes, and heroines are not dead. We who are alive today constantly speak, hear, write, and read their names, even if we don't always know it.

Echo, for example, is an echo of a story three millennia old. Echo was a beautiful nymph who once upon a time aided Zeus in a love affair by keeping his wife, Hera, occupied in conversation. As a punishment for such verbal meddling, Hera confiscated Echo's power to initiate conversation and allowed her to repeat only the last words of anything she heard.

Such was a sorry enough fate, but later Echo fell madly in love with a smashingly handsome demigod, Narcissus, who, because of Echo's peculiar handicap, would have nothing to do with her. So deeply did the nymph grieve for her unrequited love that she wasted away until nothing was left but her voice, always repeating the last words she heard.

The fate that befell Narcissus explains why his name has been transformed into words like *narcissism* and *narcissistic*, pertaining to extreme self-love. One day Narcissus looked into a still forest lake and beheld his own face for the first time, although he did not know it was his. He at once fell in love with the beautiful image, and he, like Echo, pined away for a love that could never be consummated.

A pantheon of gods, goddesses, heroes, and fabulous creatures inhabit the world of classical mythology and the words that echo them:

One of the vilest of mythology's villains was King Tantalus, who served the body of his young son to the gods for dinner. They soon discovered the king's atrocity, restored the dead boy to life, and devised an eternal punishment for the heinous crime. They banished the king to Hades, where he was condemned to stand in a sparkling pool of water with boughs of luscious fruit overhead. When he stooped to drink, the water drained away through the bottom of the pool, and when he wished to eat, the branches of fruit swayed just out of his grasp. Ever since, when something presents itself temptingly to our view, we invoke this king's name: *tantalize*.

A dreadful monster called the Minotaur lived in a labyrinth on the island of Crete. Theseus, the founder-king of Athens, volunteered to enter the labyrinth and slay the beast in order to stanch the constant slaughter of Athenian youth fed to the creature. Ariadne, the daughter of the Cretan king, had fallen in love with Theseus and provided him with a clewe (Middle English), a ball of thread, that he unwound as he went into the maze. After Theseus decapitated the Minotaur, the thread guided him out of the heart of the maze.

So the first clue was a simple ball of yarn, but gradually *clewe*, now *clue*, came to mean anything that helps us to solve a baffling situation, something that leads us from the unknown to the known.

An adjective that means "merry, inspiring mirth" comes from the name the ancient Romans gave to Jove, the king of their gods, because it was a happy omen to be born under his influence: *jovial*.

The frenetic Greek nature god Pan was said to cause sudden fear by darting out from behind bushes and terrifying passers-by. That fear now bears his name: *panic*.

Aphrodite, the goddess of love and beauty, called Venus by the Romans, bequeaths us many words, including *aphrodisiac, hermaphrodite, venereal,* and *venerate*.

A God is Hiding in Your Sentence

A mighty Greek hero needed all his power to complete twelve exceedingly laborious labors, everything from battling fearsome creatures to clearing stables of bovine dung. We use a form of his name to describe a prodigious effort or an extraordinarily difficult task: *herculean*.

Something that is *titanic* possesses great power and size. The word descends from the Titans, a race of Greek mythological giants. The titan Atlas was tasked with holding up the heavens. Starting in the sixteenth century, books of maps featured on their covers the giant with the weight of the weight of the world on his shoulders with the title *Atlas*.

A tribe of female warriors cut off their right breasts in order to handle their bows more efficiently. The name of their tribe originally meant "breastless"; it now means "a powerful woman": *amazon*.

Because of its fluidity and mobility, quicksilver is identified by a more common label that is the Roman name for the Greek god Hermes, the winged messenger of the gods, better known as Mercury. That name has also bequeathed us an adjective meaning "swift, eloquent, volatile": *mercury, mercurial*.

In Greco-Roman mythology Hephaestus is the god of blacksmiths, metalworkers, artisans, and fire. The Romans dubbed him *Vulcanus*, which spews out our word *volcano*.

Pandora was the first woman. The gods gave her a box and warned her not to open it. Unable to contain her curiosity, Pandora did open the box and out flew all the troubles that plague humankind. Only hope remained. As a result of this anti-feminist story, a *Pandora's box* has come to denote "a source of evil that should be contained."

A mnemonic device is a shortcut memory aid to remembrance of things fast and accurately. *Mnemonic* (the *m* is silent) is eponymously derived from Mnemosyne, the shadowy daughter of Uranus and Gaea, a wife of Zeus, and mother of the nine muses. Mnemosyne caught Zeus's eye when he decided that he wanted to record, so that people would remember, the triumphs of the gods.

The most common mnemonic device is an acrostic-style sentence in which the first letter of each word triggers the name of each item to be memorized, as in "Will A Jolly Man Make A Jolly Visitor?" In order, each first letter is the first letter of the last name of our first eight presidents: Washington, Adams, Jefferson, Madison, Monroe, Adams, Jackson, Van Buren.

In Homer's *Iliad,* the Greek herald Stentor was a human public address system, for his voice could be heard all over camp. Today, the adjective form of his name means "loud-voiced, bellowing.": *stentorian.*

The greatest Greek warrior in the *Iliad* was Achilles. When he was an infant, his mother dipped him into the river Styx to make him invulnerable, except for his heel, with which she grasped him. Ultimately, Achilles was slain when Paris shot him in the heel with a poisoned arrow. That's why a weak spot is often called *an Achilles heel.*

The most famous of all of Homer's creations, Odysseus, spent ten years after the fall of Troy wandering through the ancient world encountering sorceresses, Sirens, and Cyclopes. The wily hero's name lives on in the word we use to describe a long journey or voyage marked by bizarre turns of events: *odyssey.*

The nine Muses, all daughters of Zeus, were the personification of the arts, including dance, theater, poetry, and musical instruments. From the Muses we inherit the words *music* and *museum.*

☺Mythic Riddles

I don't know much about Greek mythology. It's my Achilles elbow.

But I do know enough to lay some mythological riddles on you. The most famous riddle of all is the one that the Sphinx put to Oedipus: "What goes on four legs in the morning, on two at noon and on three at night?" Oedipus, one of the first game-show contestants, answered: "Man. In infancy, he crawls. In his prime, he walks. In old age, he leans on a staff." He was correct and thus became Oedipus Rex.

As a more modern riddle asks: What's the difference between a centaur and a senator?

Answer: One is half man and half horse's ass—and the other is a creature in mythology.

The humor in that riddle is side splitting, knee slapping, and gut busting if, from your knowledge of Greek mythology, you are able to conjure an image of a centaur—equine in the nether regions but possessing the head, arms, and torso of a human being.

What is a Cyclops's favorite song?

Answer: "I Only Have Eye for You."

The punch line is most effective if you know that the Cyclopes sported only one eye in the middle of their forehead (and thus had 20 vision).

Please take a minotaur two to visit my exhibition of mythic riddles about Greek gods, goddesses, heroes, and monsters.

Summarize Greek mythology in five words. *"Unfortunately, Zeus was feeling horny."*

What is the main drain on Zeus's bank account? *Child support.*

What does Zeus wear under his clothes? *Thunderwear.*

What did Zeus say to Athena when she sprang from his head in full armor? *"Girl, you are really getting on Minerva."*

What do you call the goddess of knowledge when she has no friends? *Pal-less Athena.*

How to Greek women prepare for a toga party? *They make a Hera pointment.*

Why doesn't Aphrodite date tennis players? *Because love means nothing to them.*

What Roman god can referee a tennis match without having to turn back and forth? *Janus. He has two faces that look in opposite directions.*

What carry-out meal is evil? *Pandora's box lunch.*

What Greek figure started a new kind of music? *Sisyphus. He was the first rock and roller.*

Why did the Cyclops couple get along so well? *They saw eye to eye on everything.*

In Greek mythology, who are the angriest goddesses? *The three Furies.*

What mythological monster always had a bad-hair day? *Medusa.*

What is Medusa's favorite cheese? *Gorgonzola.*

Why would Prometheus be a good mailman? *Because the job involves de-livering.*

What kind of horse was the Trojan horse? *A phony pony that turned into a night mare.*

Which Greek hero was in need of a podiatrist? *Achilles. He was weak in the heel.*

What do Achilles and an honest politician have in common? *They're both imaginary people.*

Mythic Riddles

What games did the children of the Greek gods play? *Hydra go seek and pick up Styx.*

What do Greeks use to sculpt statues of their mythological gods and heroes? *Con-Crete.*

It's About Time

In his tragedy *Romeo and Juliet,* William Shakespeare speaks of people who "run before the clock," as if the hands of the clock would sweep them away if they didn't get a move on. More than a half-century later, in his poem "To His Coy Mistress," Andrew Marvell writes, "But at my back I always hear / Time's wingèd chariot hurrying near."

The Oxford list of word frequencies in English confirms this obsession with time and productivity by revealing that *time* is the most frequently used noun in our language. *Year* is ranked third, *day* fifth, and *week* seventeenth. Nowadays, so many of us seem to be running harder, working harder, and taking fewer and shorter vacations.

So it's about time to talk about time. Do you ever wonder where the names of our months come from? The answer is three sources—Greek and Roman deities, Roman rulers, and numbers:

January is "the month of Janus," the Roman god of beginnings and endings. *Janus* presided over doors and gates, appropriate for the ending of one year and the beginning of the next. Indeed, Janus was usually depicted with two faces, one looking backward and one forward.

In our English language repose about fifty words and compounds that we call Janus-faced words because they contain two opposite meaning. When the sun or stars are out, they are visible, but when the lights are out, they are invisible. Other Janus-faced words (also known as contronyms) include *hold up,* "to support"/"to hinder"; *buckle* "to fasten together"/ "to fall apart"; and *scan*, "to examine carefully"/"to glance at hastily."

February is the month of cleansing, from *februa*, the name of Roman purification festival held the thirteenth through the fifteenth of this month. This festival suppressed evil spirits, purified the city, and released health and fertility.

Which god gets a planet *and* a month named after him? Mars. In ancient Rome, several festivals of Mars took place in March because that was the earliest month of the year when the weather was mild enough to start a war. At one time, March was the first month in the Roman calendar.

April may derive from the Latin *Apru*, a reference to the Greek goddess Aphrodite. Or the month may grow out of the Latin *aperio*, meaning "to open," referring to the floral buds starting to open during that month.

The month of *May* may spring from the ancient Roman goddess Maia, sometime wife of Vulcan and mother of Mercury. (She's often conflated with a Greek mountain nymph/ goddess of the same name.) Roman Maia was a nurturer and an earth goddess, connected with warmth, growth, and increase, which explains her connection with springtime, when flowers and crops burst forth.

June descends from the ancient Roman goddess Juno, wife of Jupiter and goddess of marriage and childbirth. The Romans traditionally married in June to honor Juno and ensure an auspicious union. That custom continues today.

July is the first month in the calendar that bears the name of a real person, Julius Caesar, rather than a deity. July is the month of his birth. Caesar, dictator of Rome, directed the development of the Julian calendar, which divided the year into twelve months of thirty or thirty-one days, except for February, with either twenty-eight or twenty-nine days. This calendar was a major improvement on the older Roman calendar and served as the basis for our current Gregorian calendar. Caesar renamed Quintilus, the fifth month, after himself.

A second Roman ruler is enshrined in *August*. Gaius Julius Caesar (born Gaius Octavius Thurinus), the great nephew and adopted son and heir of Julius Caesar, became the first emperor of Rome. The Roman Senate bestowed the name Augustus on him, which gave rise to the adjective *august*, "respected and impressive." Following his great uncle's lead, he renamed *Sextilis*, the sixth month, after himself.

September, with its derivation from the Latin *septem*, looks as if it should be the seventh month of the year. And October *(octo)*, November *(novem)*, and December *(decem)* appear in their structure to be the eighth, ninth, and tenth months. And they once were, when the Roman lunar calendar started the year in March.

But all that changed in 46 BCE, when a previously unnamed span of time was dubbed January and February, the first two months of the new Julian calendar, making September, October, November, and December the ninth, tenth, eleventh, and twelfth months of the year.

Not only do you measure your life month by month. You live your life day by day, through moody Mondays, hump-day Wednesdays, and TGI Fridays, over and over and over again. Who designed this scheme, and how did these names come about?

The Babylonians, avid astronomers and astrologers, created the seven-day week and named those days after the seven "planets" visible to the naked eye, which had been named after gods and one goddess—the Sun, the Moon, Mercury, Venus, Mars, Jupiter, and Saturn. The Greeks followed suit with a seven-day week, naming the days after the planets.

When the Romans shifted from an eight-day week to a seven-day week as a feature of their calendar in the first century BCE, they translated and adopted the names for the days that the Greeks had created.

Language often follows armies. The Romans marched north and battled various Germanic tribes between 113 BCE and 596 CE. Among other words, they carried the names of the days with them, which again were translated by the native tribes.

Of course, some tribes fought back. Around 450 CE, the Germanic Anglo-Saxons ousted the Romans from Britain. At the same time, the Germanic names for the days ousted the Roman names in that area.

For example, the Greek term *hēmērāHēlíou* (day of the Sun) became the Latin *diēsSōlis*. That became the Anglo-Saxon (Old English) word *Sunnandæg* (Sun's day), then *Sunedai*, and, finally, Sunday, sometime around 1250 CE.

The other six days of the week underwent similar transitions:

Modern English	**Greek**	**Latin**	**Old English**
Monday (day of the Moon)	*hēmērāSelḗnēs*	*diēsLūnae*	*Mōnandæg*
Tuesday (day of Mars)	*hēmērāÁreōs)*	*diēsM8rtis*	*Tīwesdæg*
Wednesday (day of Mercury)	*hēmērāHermoû*	*diēsMercuri8*	*Wōdnesdæg*
Thursday (day of Jupiter)	*hēmērāDiós*	*diēsIovis*	*Þūnresdæg*
Friday (day of Venus)	*hēmērāAphrodítēs*	*diēsVeneris*	*Frīgedæg*
Saturday (day of Saturn)	*hēmērāKrónou*	*diēsSaturnī*	*Sæturnesdæg*

And there you have it: a twelve-month, fifty-two-week calendar of word origins to see you through the whole year.

SACRED WORDS

That Old-Time Religion

We think of carnivals as traveling entertainments with rides, sideshows, games, cotton candy, and balloons. But the first carnivals were pre-Lenten celebrations—a last fling before penitence. The Latin word parts *carne*, "meat, flesh," and *vale*, "farewell," indicate that the earliest carnivals were seasons of feasting and merrymaking, "a farewell to meat" just before Lent.

Why can *story* mean both "a tale" and "the level of a building"? Both words come down to us from the Latin *historia*, "to know," and French *histoire*, where it means both "a tale" and "history." The endurance of the meanings "tale" and "floor" is architectural. Back in the Middle Ages, it was the custom in many parts of Europe to paint scenes depicting historical, legendary, biblical, or literary subjects on the outside of the various floors of buildings. Each level represented a story, and, before long, the levels themselves were called stories.

Religion, derived from the Latin *religionem,* "respect for what is sacred," "to bind fast," binds people together and with God or gods and influences a great many lives and the words we speak and hear and write and read every day. *Story* is one of many words and expressions that began in religion. Because our society has become secularized, we overlook the religious foundation of our daily parlance:

The literal meaning of *atone* issues from what the word actually looks like—to be "at one," that is, united with God.

Bonfires were originally the bone fires that consumed the bodies of saints who were burned during the English Reformation.

Enthusiastic, from the Greek *enthusiasmos,* "a god within," first meant "filled with God," as did *giddy,* from Anglo Saxon *gydig,* "god-held man."

The Latin word for "cross," *crux,* is embedded in the words *crux, crucial, cruise, crusade,* and *excruciating,* which has broadened from denoting the agony of the crucifixion to any kind of torturous pain.

Fan, is a clipping of *fanatic,* from the Latin *fanaticus,* "inspired by the temple." The opposite, *profane,* describes a person who is irreverent, from the Latin *pro,* "outside," and *fanum,* "the temple."

Our traditional farewell, *good-bye,* turns out to be a shortening of the sentence "God be with you."

In its original meaning, an *icon* was a small religious painting used as an aid to devotion. In its new meaning, icons are now people who achieve superstar status in the worlds of politics, sports, the arts and entertainment. Many consider this change to be a debasement of a perfectly good word.

A *red-letter day* is so-called because of the practice of calendar and almanac publishers of printing the numbers of saints' days and religious feast days in red ink. Such days now describe any distinctive day in a person's life, such as birthdays, graduations, and the day the local sports team wins a championship.

In bygone days, political offenders, military captives, and heretics were executed almost out of hand. There was but a thin pretense of justice in which the prisoner could confess (*shrive*) his sins to a priest and prepare his soul for death. Those who kept these unfortunate souls in thrall often allotted but a short time for confession, and this hurried procedure became known as *short shrift.* Nowadays, this compound means "to give scant attention, to make quick work of."

The True Meanings of Christmas

The great English etymologist Owen Barfield once wrote, "Words may be made to disgorge the past that is bottled up inside of them, as coal and wine, when we kindle or drink them, yield up their bottled sunshine." When we uncap the sunshine that is stored inside the many words that relate to the Christmas season, we discover that the light that streams forth illuminates centuries of human history and customs.

The word *Christmas* derives from the Old English *Cristes Maesse*, meaning "the festival mass of Christ." *Christmas* is a fine example of a disguised compound, a word formed from two independent morphemes (meaning-bearing elements) that have become so closely welded together that their individual identities have been lost.

Turns out that the word *holiday* is another disguised compound, descending from the Old English *haligdaeg*, "holy day." With the change in pronunciation has come a change in meaning so that holidays, such as Independence Day and Labor Day, are not necessarily holy. The *day* in *holiday* has also been transmuted so that an American can enjoy a three-day holiday.

The name *Christ* is a translation of the Hebrew word *messiah*, "the anointed one," rendered through the Greek as Christós. *Jesus* also reaches back to the ancient Hebrew name Yeshua, one of the names for God.

We learn about Jesus through the *gospels*. *Gospel* is yet another disguised compound, from the Old English *god*, "good," and *spel*, "news." The gospels of Matthew, Mark, Luke, and John spread the good news of the life and work of Christ. No surprise then that the four men who wrote the gospels are called *evangelists,* from the Greek *euaggelion,* which also means "good news."

The babe was born in *Bethlehem,* a Hebrew word meaning "house of bread." The Christ child was laid in a *manger,* a word related to the French verb *manger,* "to eat." Why? Because Jesus's crib was a large wooden box that usually served as a trough for feeding cattle.

We call the worship of the newborn babe the *Adoration,* from the Latin *adoratio*: *ad-*"to," and *oro* – "pray"; hence, "to pray to." Among those who came to worship were wise men from the East, *magi,* a Latin word for "magician" or "astrologer." The number of wise men is never mentioned in the gospels; we infer three from the gifts bestowed on the Christ child.

The Greek letter *chi,* spelled with an *X,* is the first letter of the word *Xristos,* which is Greek for Christ. *Xmas,* then, is actually a Greek derivative that does not eradicate the name of Christ from *Christmas.* The name of the holiday has been abbreviated as *Xmas* for five hundred years. Slogans like "Put the Christ back in Christmas" were coined by people who don't know the history of *X.* No offense intended then or now by the *X.*

Yuletide as a synonym for the Christmas season dates back to a pagan and then Christian period of feasting about the time of the winter solstice, December 22. The origin of *yule* is uncertain. One suggestion is that *yule* comes from the Gothic *giul* or *hiul,* which meant "wheel." In this context, *yule* signifies that the sun, like a wheel, has completed its annual journey. Whence the *tide* in *Yuletide*? From an Old English word meaning "time," as in *Eastertide.*

Christmas occurs shortly after the winter solstice, when the sun reaches its most southerly excursion relative to the celestial equator. The winter solstice enfolds the longest night of the year, just before the days slowly fill back up with brightness.

At the time of the summer and winter solstices, the sun, before journeying back toward the equator, appears to stand still. This phenomenon is reflected in the Latin roots of the word: *sol,* meaning "sun," and *sistere,* "to stand still."

The True Meanings of Christmas

Among the most fascinating Christmas etymologies are those for *Santa Claus* and *Kris Kringle*. When the Dutch came to the New World during the seventeenth century, the figure of Saint Nikolaas, their patron saint, was on the first ship. After the Dutch lost control of New Amsterdam, *Sinterklaas* (a form of *Saint Nikolaas*) became anglicized into *Santa Claus*.

Kris Kringle reflects an even more drastic change from one language to another. Immigrants from the Holy Roman Empire (now Germany, Austria, and Switzerland) settled in Pennsylvania in the seventeenth and eighteenth centuries. They held the custom that the Christ Child, "the Christ-kinkle," brought gifts for the children on Christmas Eve. When English-speaking settlers moved near these Pennsylvania Dutch (also known as Pennsylvania Deutsch), the Christ-kinkle became *Kris Kringle*. By the 1840s, Kris Kringle had irretrievably taken on the identity of St. Nicholas, or Santa Claus.

The word *carol* comes from the Greek word *choraulein*, "to accompany a chorus on a reed instrument." The word transmogrified to *carol* and came to signify a round dance. People originally performed carols on several occasions during the year. By the 1600s, carols involved singing only, and Christmas had become the main holiday for these songs.

Of the various plants associated with the Christmas season, the poinsettia possesses the most intriguing history etymologically. A Mexican legend tells of a penniless boy who presented to the Christ Child a beautiful plant with scarlet leaves that resembled the Star of Bethlehem. The Mexicans named the plant *Flor de la Noche Buena*, "Christmas Eve Flower." Dr. Joel Roberts Poinsett, the first U.S. minister to Mexico, came upon the red and green Christmas plant there in 1828 and brought it to the United States, where it was named in his honor in 1836. The poinsettia has become one of the most popular of Christmas plants—and one of the most misspelled words (*pointsettia, pointsetta, poinsetta*) in the English language.

Another botanical Christmas item is the pear tree. In the seasonal song "The Twelve Days of Christmas," have you ever wondered why the true love sends not only a partridge but also an entire pear tree? That's because in the early French version of the song the suitor gave only a partridge, which in French is rendered as *une pertriz*. A 1718 English version combined the two—"a partridge, *une pertriz*"—which, slightly corrupted, came out sounding like "a partridge in a pear tree." Ever since, the partridge has remained proudly perched in a pear tree.

A Merry Christ Mass and Happy Holy Days to all!

Gee Whiz!

English speakers apparently take deeply to heart the biblical commandment not to use the Lord's name in vain and Christ's injunction to eschew all swearing, either by heaven or by earth.

We live in a culture in which calling out the name of Jesus Christ in church is a sign of moral rectitude. But, once outside, we have to find ways of not quite saying that name. Most prominent among those taboo euphemisms, as they are called, are *gee, geez,* and *gee whiz (Jesus)*. Add to that list *gee whillikers, geez Louise, jesum crow, Christmas, holy cow, holy crow, holy Christmas, cripes, criminey, crikey, by Jingo, by Jiminy, Jiminy Cricket, Jiminy Christmas, Judas Priest,* and even *jeepers creepers.*

These linguistic strategies have been labeled "taboo euphemisms" and "taboo deformations." Have you ever noticed how many different ways we've come up with to avoid saying *God* and *damnation?*: *gosh, golly, goodness gracious, good grief, good gravy, dad gum it, by gar, by golly, by gum, dad gum, doggone, gol dang, gol darn, dear me* (an approximation of the Italian *Dio mio,* "my God"), *jumpin' Jehoshaphat* ("jumping Jehovah"), *begorrah* (Irish for "by God"), *great Scott, gosh all fishhooks* ("God almighty"), *by gorey, by Godfrey,* W.C. Fields' *Godfrey Daniels, good gravy,* and *what in tarnation* ("damnation")!

More antique and elegant stratagems for skirting the name of the Almighty include *egad* ("ye gods"), *odds bodkins* (a shortening of "God's body"), *gadzooks* ("God's hooks," the nails of the cross), *drat* ("God rot"), *'sblood* ("God's blood"), and *zounds* ("God's wounds").

Who needs to shout, "Hell!" when Sam Hill (euphemism for "damn hell") is available to help us cuss (*curse*) in a socially acceptable manner? Sam Hill was not a particular person, but "Sam Hill" expressions, such as *what the Sam Hill!* and *mad as Sam Hill,* grew up in the American West in the 1830s. Sam Hill was a trusty friend of frontiersmen, especially when they needed to clean up their language in the presence of womenfolk. Additional surrogates for *hell* flame up as *heck, hey, Halifax, Hoboken,* and *Jesse* ("if you don't watch out, you're going to catch Jesse").

😃Name That Tune!

The word *bible* derives from the Greek *biblia*, which means "books." Indeed, the Bible is a whole library of books that contain many different kinds of literature—history, narrative, short stories, poetry, philosophy, riddles, fables, allegories, letters, and drama. Many parts of the Bible are highly dramatic because they show in detail the sweep of grand events as experienced by a vivid and diverse cast of persons.

In 2017, after fifty-six years representing the city where I live, the San Diego Chargers betrayed our trust and skulked away to Los Angeles. Instantly, the football team was dubbed the Los Angeles Judases. Most of us San Diego sports fans understood the biblical allusion because, reflecting the New Testament narrative about Judas Iscariot's betrayal of Jesus Christ, a traitorous man is now called a Judas.

As their hopes and fears, ambitions and tragedies, and laughter and sorrows unfold in the Bible, many of these men and women have become so familiar to so many readers that their names have become archetypal. Thus, a large man is a Goliath, an old man a Methuselah, a wise man a Solomon, an evil woman a Jezebel, a doer of good deeds a Good Samaritan, a long-suffering man a Job, a skeptical man a Doubting Thomas, a mighty hunter a Nimrod, and a strong man a Samson.

Here's a playlist of theme songs. Match each biblical personage with his or her appropriate popular song. *Examples:* Shadrach, Meshach, and Abednego's song would be "Great Balls of Fire!" owing to their placement into a fiery furnace by Nebuchadnezzar

II in the Book of Daniel. Conversely, Eliphaz, Bildad, and Zophar's, who advised a blameless Job to repent, would be paired with "Cold Comfort."

1. Absalom — "Blinded By the Light"
2. Adam and Eve — "Coat of Many Colors"
3. Bathsheba — "Crying Over You"
4. Cain — "Do It Now, Do It Good"
5. Daniel — "Hair"
6. David — "I Could Have Danced All Night"
7. Esther — "I Feel Pretty"
8. The Good Samaritan — "I Got You Babe"
9. Jezebel — "I'm Sorry"
10. Job — "The Lady Is a Tramp"
11. John the Baptist — "Let's Hear It For the Boy"
12. Jonah — "The Lion Sleeps Tonight"
13. Joseph — "Losing My Head Over You"
14. Lazarus — "Psycho Killer"
15. The Magi — "Raindrops Keep Fallin' On My Head"
16. Mary Magdalene — "Rebel, Rebel"
17. Methuselah — "The Second Time Around"
18. Moses — "Shadow of a Doubt"
19. Noah — "Starry Starry Night"
20. Paul — "Stayin' Alive"
21. Peter — "Strangers in Paradise"
22. Pharaoh's daughter — "The Wanderer"
23. Salome — "A Whale Of a Tale"
24. Samson — "Why's Everybody Always Picking on Me?"
25. Thomas — "Your Cheatin' Heart"

Name That Tune!

Answers

1. Absalom: "Rebel, Rebel" 2. Adam and Eve: "Strangers in Paradise" 3. Bathsheba: "Your Cheatin' Heart" 4. Cain: "Psycho Killer" 5. Daniel: "The Lion Sleeps Tonight"

6. David: "Let's Hear It For the Boy" 7. Esther: "I Feel Pretty" 8. The Good Samaritan: "Do It Now, Do It Good" 9. Jezebel: "The Lady is a Tramp" 10. Job: "Why's Everybody Always Picking on Me?"

11. John the Baptist: "Losing My Head Over You" 12. Jonah: "A Whale Of a Tale" 13. Joseph: "Coat of Many Colors" 14. Lazarus: "The Second Time Around" 15. The Magi: "Starry Starry Night"

16. Mary Magdalene: "Crying Over You" 17. Methuselah: "Stayin' Alive" 18. Moses: "The Wanderer" 19. Noah: "Raindrops Keep Fallin' On My Head" 20. Paul: "Blinded By the Light"

21. Peter: "I'm Sorry" 22. Pharaoh's daughter: "I Got You Babe" 23. Salome: "I Could Have Danced All Night" 24. Samson: "Hair" (could also be Absalom) 25. Thomas: "Shadow of a Doubt"

☺Bible Riddles

Riddles are perhaps the most ancient of all verbal puzzles, dating back at least twenty-five hundred years. In the book of Judges, the mighty Samson comes upon a swarm of bees making honey in the carcass of a lion. From this, Samson makes a bet with the Philistines that they cannot solve his riddle: "Out of the eater came something to eat. Out of the strong came something sweet." After seven days of weeping, Samson's wife wheedles the answer out of him and conveys it to the Philistines. In a rage, Samson kills thirty of them and lays waste their city.

These days, we don't take riddles quite as seriously, but we do derive sweetness and strength from a cleverly turned poser. Gaze upon modern riddles about four Old Testament personages—Adam and Eve, Noah, and Moses:

At what time of day was Adam created? *A little before Eve.*
Who was the champion runner of all time? *Adam. He was first in the human race.*
Why were Adam and Eve the happiest couple in history? *Because Eve couldn't tell Adam how many other men she could have married, and Adam couldn't tell Eve how much he loved his mother's cooking.*
Why were Adam and Eve kicked out of the Garden of Eden? *Because they were the first to ignore Apple terms & conditions.*
What excuse did Adam give to his children as to why he no longer lived in Eden? *"Your mother ate us out of house and home."*
What was the longest day in the Bible? *The one with no Eve.*
Why couldn't Eve have measles? *Because she'd Adam.*

Did Eve ever have a date with Adam? *No, it was an apple.*

How were Adam and Eve prevented from gambling? *They lost their paradise.*

What did Adam and Eve never have but left to their children? *Belly buttons.*

What evidence is there that Adam and Eve were pretty noisy? *They raised Cain.*

When is meat first mentioned in the Bible? *When Noah took Ham onto the ark.*

Where did Noah keep the bees? *In the ark hives.*

Why couldn't people play cards on the ark? *Noah sat on the deck.*

Why couldn't Noah catch many fish? *He only had two worms.*

Who were the best financiers in the Bible? *Noah, who floated his stock while the whole world was in liquidation, and Pharaoh's daughter, who took a little prophet from the rushes on the banks.*

Who was the first man in the Bible to use a computer? *Moses. He downloaded data from the cloud to his tablet.*

How does Moses make his coffee? *Hebrews it.*

Who was the first man in the Bible to break all Ten Commandments? *Moses.*

How do we know for certain that Moses was a male? *He spent forty years wandering in the desert and never stopped to ask for directions.*

Who were the three most constipated men in the Bible? *Cain, because he wasn't Abel; Methuselah, who sat on the throne for nine-hundred years; and Moses, because God gave him two tablets and sent him into the wilderness.*

Location, Location

HAMBURG, GERMANY

HAMBURGER

FRANKFURT, GERMANY

FRANKFURTER

Putting Words In Their Places

Like the names of people, place names have similarly enriched the English language with many common words. An atlas of cities, towns, regions, and nations have become eponymously enshrined in our dictionaries, usually as uncapitalized nouns, verbs, or adjectives. We put words in their places and places in our words.

In order to spend more uninterrupted time at the gambling tables, John Montagu, Fourth Earl of Sandwich ("sand village"), ordered his servants to bring him an impromptu meal of slices of beef slapped between two slices of bread. Thus, America's favorite luncheon repast was rustled up to feed a nobleman's gambling addiction.

Somebody once defined a hamburger as "a humble immigrant hunk of meat that came to this country from Germany and soared to fame on a bun." That somebody was perfectly right. In its native land the dish was originally called "Hamburg steak," taking its name from the West German city of Hamburg.

After the Hamburg steak arrived in the United States midway through the last century with the first great wave of German immigrants, its name began to change. Ultimately the Hamburg steak dropped its capital *H*, acquired the suffix – *er*, lost the *steak*, and moved from the platter to the plane between two slices of baked dough. Voila: a hamburger!

The adventure in word evolution didn't stop there. Somewhere along the way, speakers of English liberally interpreted *burger* to mean "sandwich made with a bun." Once *burger* became a new word part, *cheeseburger, beefburger, baconburger, fishburger, chiliburger,* and a tray full of other burgers entered the American scene and gullet.

Frankfurter, which takes its name from Frankfurt, Germany, has traveled the same linguistic road. *Furter* is now used to denote almost any kind of sandwich with protein slapped inside an elongated bun, as in *chickenfurter* and *fishfurter*.

And speaking of frankfurters, do you know that Charlemagne mustered his Franks and set out with great relish to assault and pepper his enemies, but he couldn't ketchup? Frankly, I never sausage a pun. It's the wurst!

Let's chew on another sandwich. In days of yore, back in the Middle AgesmI was born and grew up in Philadelphia a coon's age and a month of Sundays ago—when Hector was a pup and dinosaurs roamed the earth. *Phillufia,* or *Philly,* which is what we kids called the city, was where the epicurean delight made with cold cuts, cheese, tomatoes, pickles, peppers, and onions stuffed into a long, hard-crusted Italian bread loaf was invented.

The creation of that sandwich took place in the Italian pushcart section of the city, known as Hog Island. Some linguists contend that *Hog Island* easily transmogrified into *hoagie,* while others claim that the label *hoagie* arose because only a hog had the appetite or the technique to eat one properly.

As a young adult I moved to northern New England ("N'Hampsha," to be specific), where the same sandwich designed to be a meal in itself is called a grinder, because you need a good set of grinders to chew them. But my travels around the United States have revealed that the hoagie or grinder is called at least a dozen other names—a *bomber, Garibaldi* (after the Italian liberator), *hero, Italian sandwich, rocket, sub, submarine* (which is what they call it in California, where I now live), *torpedo, wedge, wedgie,* and, in the deep South, a *poor-boy* (usually pronounced "poh-boy").

These yummy sandwiches only begin to illustrate the place that places have in our language:

A *bikini* is a skimpy, two-piece swimsuit named after the Bikini atoll in the Pacific Marshall Islands, on which atomic bombs were tested—a truly explosive and figurative word. During the COVID-19 apocalypse, a matching medical mask and bikini top and bottom were dubbed a *trikini*.

The *limerick*, the most popular of all humorous verse forms in English, hails from a county in Ireland. One theory says that Irish mercenaries used to compose verses in that form about each other and then join in a chorus of "When we get back to Limerick town, 'twill be a glorious morning."

Blarney, which means "smooth-sounding flattery," derives from the name of a town and castle in County Cork, Ireland. An inscription on the wall of the castle proclaims that anyone brave enough to scale the wall and kiss a particular stone will be rewarded with the gift of influencing others through cajolery.

Marathon runners with bad footwear suffer the agony of defeat.

Two-and-a-half millennia ago, a little band of ten thousand Athenians defeated a host of one hundred thousand Persians at the battle of Marathon. Pheidippides, a courageous runner, brought the news of the glorious victory to Athens, which lay twenty-six miles away. He exclaimed, "Joy to you! We've won!" and died from the exertion of his immense journey. Pheidippides' heroism has inspired the *marathon*, a modern-day road race.

Nineteenth-century sailors were sometimes drugged and then forced into service on ships plying the unpopular route from San Francisco to China. From Shanghai, the name of that Chinese port we get the verb *to shanghai*, "to secure someone's services through force."

Bedlam, a contraction of "St. Mary's of Bethlehem," a sixteenth-century London hospital for the insane, has become a word for uproar or confusion.

Donnybrook, another word for disorder, in this case a wild brawl, comes down to us from the name of a fair, held in, Donnybrook, an Irish town near Dublin, infamous for its fist fights and rowdy behavior.

As an alternative to cumbersome tails on a formal full-dress dinner coat, the *tuxedo*, a tailless dinner coat, originated in

Tuxedo Junction, an exclusive community about forty miles north of New York City. This short evening coat was an immediate sensation during the Gay Nineties; it is still obligatory at many formal functions.

The Pilgrims found in America a wild fowl somewhat similar in appearance to a fowl they had known back in England—a bird that had acquired the name *turkey* because it was first imported by way of Turkey, a Middle Eastern nation that doesn't celebrate Thanksgiving nor football. Because we perceive this bird as ugly in appearance and voice, we sometimes assign its name to people we don't care for.

The inhabitants of the ancient Greek district Laconia were noted for their ability to say a lot in a few words. During a siege of their capital, a Roman general sent a note to this city's commander warning that if the Romans captured the city, they would burn it to the ground. From within the city gates came back the terse reply: "If!" The city's name lives on in the adjective *laconic*, "marked by spare speech." Sparta, a town in the district of Laconia, bequeaths us the adjective *Spartan*, "marked by strict self-discipline."

In 1516, British Lord Chancellor Sir Thomas More published *Utopia*, in which life on the island of Utopia is socially and economically ideal. The Greek etymons embedded in *Utopia* are *ou*, "not, no"; *eu*, "good," as in *eulogy* and *euphemism*; and *topos*, "place," which coalesce into "a good place that doesn't exist."

Many years ago, cloth was imported into England from Silesea, then part of Germany. The material was of such poor quality that the English referred to it contemptuously as "that cloth from Silesea," or "Silesea cloth." Ultimately the phrase was shortened even further to "sleazy cloth," and that's how *sleazy* was fabricated as a popular adjective for "cheap and shoddy." Recently the word spawned such offspring as *sleaze, sleazebag*, and *sleazeball*.

Another place name born at the tip of a pen is *Serendip*, a form of the old Arabic name for the island of Ceylon. Horace Walpole coined the word *serendipity* in his story "The Three Princes of Serendip," the heroes in which "were always making discoveries, by accident or sagacity, of things they were not in quest of." *Serendipity* is the ability to make lucky finds by accident. Many people use the word to describe any stroke of luck.

Our Native American Heritage

More than four centuries ago, the roots of Thanksgiving first took hold in our American soil. We living today commemorate the solemn dinner, back in the fall of 1621, shared by the Pilgrims of Plymouth, Massachusetts, and the Wampanoag ("Dawnlanders") Indians, the local tribe who generously pulled the fragile Pilgrim colony through their first winter and taught them how to plant corn.

Let's talk turkey about our indigenous, Native American heritage. Suppose you had been one of the early explorers or settlers of North America. You would have found many things in your new land unknown to you. The handiest way of filling voids in your vocabulary would have been to ask the locals what words they used. The early colonists began borrowing words from friendly Native Americans almost from the moment of their first contact, and many of those names have remained in our everyday language:

In a letter that British explorer John Smith wrote home in 1608, he described a critter that the Virginia Algonquians (Powhatan) called a *rahaughcum* or an *aroughcan*, "he scratches with his hands." Over the years the word was shortened and simplified to *raccoon*, one of the very first English words coined in America.

Pronouncing many of the Native American words was difficult for the early explorers and settlers. In many instances, they had to shorten and simplify the names. Identify the following animals from their Native American names:

apossoum (Don't play dead now.)
otchig (How much wood?)

Our Native American Heritage

segankw (What's black and white and stinks all over?)

The hidden animals are: *opossum* (Powhatan Algonquian), *woodchuck* (from Ojibwa Algonquian for a weasel-like fisher), and *skunk* (Abenaki Algonquian). To this menagerie we may add the likes of *caribou* (Micmac), *chipmunk* (Ojibwa), *moose* (Abenaki), and *muskrat* (Massachuset *musquash*).

You can expand the lexicon with the likes of food—*squash* (Narragansett), *pecan* (Ojibwa), *hominy* (Virginia Algonquian), *pone* (Delaware Algonquian), *pemmican* (Cree), and *succotash* (Narragansett)—and other ingredients of Native American life: *moccasin* (Narragansett), *toboggan* (Micmac Algonquian), *tomahawk* (Virginia Algonquian), *wigwam* (Abenaki), *teepee* (Dakota Siouan), *caucus* (Virginia Algonquian), *powwow* (Narragansett), *wampum* (Narragansett), *bayou* (Choctaw Muskogean), *potlatch* (Nootka), *hogan* (Navajo Athabascan), *hickory* (Virginia Algonquian), *kayak* (Inuit), *parka* (Aleut), *totem* (Ojibwa), *sachem* (Narragansett), *squaw* (Massachuset), *papoose* (Narragansett), and *mugwump* (Massachuset).

If you examine a map of the United States, you will realize how freely settlers used words of Indian origin to name the places where we live. Rivers, lakes, ponds, creeks, mountains, valleys, counties, towns, and cities as large as Chicago (from a Fox word that means "place that stinks of wild onions") bear Native American names. Four of our five Great Lakes— Huron, Ontario, Michigan, and Erie—and twenty-five of our states have names borrowed from Native American words:

Alabama: name of a tribe in the Creek Confederacy, meaning "plant cutters"; *Alaska:* "mainland" (Aleut); *Arizona:* "having a little spring" (Pima); *Arkansas:* named for the Siouan Kansa tribe (Dhegiha Siouan); *Connecticut:* "place of the long tidal river" (Southern New England Algonquian);

Idaho: "enemy" (Kiowa-Apache Athabascan); *Illinois:* "he speaks the typical way" (Ottawa from Miami-Illinois); *Iowa:* "sleepy ones" (Santee Siouan); *Kansas:* named for the Siouan Kansa tribe (Dhegiha Siouan); *Kentucky:* "meadowland" (Wyandot Iroquoian);

Massachusetts: "great hillock place" (Massachusett); *Michigan:* "great water (Ojibwa); *Minnesota:* "milky blue river" (Dakota); *Mississippi:* "large river" (Ottawa); *Missouri:* "wood boat, dugout" (Miami-Illinois);

Nebraska: "flat water" (Omaha Siouan); *North Dakota* and *South Dakota:* "friendly," "allies" (Dakota Siouan); *Ohio:* "great river" (Seneca Iroquoian); *Oklahoma:* "red people" (Choctaw);

Tennessee: "name of a Cherokee village"; *Texas:* "friends, allies" (Caddo); *Utah:* named after the tribe Ute, "high" (Western Apache); *Wisconsin:* "It lies red," referring to the Wisconsin River (Miami-Illinois); *Wyoming:* "at the big river flat" (Munsee).

Some of our loveliest place names began life as Native American words—*Susquehanna* (Algonquian), *Shenandoah* (Oneida), and *Rappahannock* (Delaware). Such names are the stuff of poetry. To the poet Walt Whitman, *Monongahela* (Unami Delaware) "rolls with venison richness upon the palate." About the Lenape Indians William Penn wrote: "I know not a language spoken in Europe that hath words of more sweetness and greatness." How fortunate we are that the poetry the First Peoples heard in the American landscape lives on in our American language.

☺Puns That Babylon

I'm a member of the Flat Earth Society. We have chapters around the globe. I'm also a member of the Round Earth Society. Our chapters extend to the four corners of the Earth.

We hear a lot these days about geographical illiteracy, the inability of Americans to name the capital of their state or to locate Afghanistan or even the Pacific Ocean on a world map. As an antidote to such spatial ignorance, here's a chance for you to increase your geographical knowledge as well as your skill in fabricating outrageous puns.

Complete each statement below with the name of a country or republic in the list that follows. Each item appears just once in the answers at the end of the game. *Example:* Wear your winter coat today, or you'll get <u>Chile</u>. *Another example:* I hope you'll enjoy playing this punderful game and won't <u>Crimea</u> river about it.

Belgium	Hungary	Rumania
Bolivia	India	Russia
Brazil	Iran	Saudi
China	Iraq	Senegal
Cuba	Israel	Spain
Denmark	Jamaica	Sudan
Egypt	Kenya	Sweden
England	Laos	Syria
France	Norway	Tibet
Germany	Pakistan	Turkey
Greece	Panama	Ukraine
Haiti	Peru	Uruguay
Holland	Poland	Wales

Richard Lederer

1. I'm not kidding. I'm _____s.
2. You stood still, but _____.
3. I'm between _____ and a hard place.
4. Save the _____ before they become extinct.
5. I don't _____ broke my expensive _____ vase.

6. I'll _____ board in two.
7. Alco_____ cigarettes are bad habits.
8. Don't put the chair in the study, Mark. Put it in the _____.
9. Give me a good _____ I'll be willing _____ that I can vault fifteen feet.
10. Little Miss Muffet liked neither curds _____.

11. Your leather wallet is fake, but mine _____.
12. Your backpack is brown, but my back_____.
13. Your zebra is healthy, but my ze_____.
14. A strong antibody will defeat a _____ time.
15. I'm a gal, and _____, and you've never _____ like me.

16. I see your daughter is taking piano lessons. _____ do it?
17. As soil erosion increases, we keep los_____.
18. I love coffee, but I _____. Please give me a _____ sugar to _____ my coffee.
19. That rotten _____. _____ me.
20. Dan's car plowed into mine, so I'm going to _____.

21. On Thanksgiving I get _____ for _____, if it doesn't have too much _____.
22. If you are obsessed with kangaroos, you have kanga_____.
23. I can't figure out what's causing thi_____ in my elbow.
24. If _____ your neck, you'll be able to see over the fence.
25. The sun will come up when it comes up. You can't _____ sunrise.

26. You've been acting crazy. I wonder what's gotten _____.
27. If you can pan a pa, I can _____.
28. With _____ like these, who needs enemies?
29. Please be quiet so that I can _____se this book.
30. Hey, Jim. _____ please ring the _____?

Answers

1. Syria 2. Iran 3. Iraq 4. Wales 5. Bolivia / China

6. Saudi 7. Holland 8. Denmark 9. Poland / Tibet 10. Norway

11. Israel 12. Pakistan 13. Brazil 14. Germany 15. Uruguay / Senegal

16. Jamaica 17. England 18. Haiti / Cuba / Sweden 19. Laos / Egypt 20. Sudan

21. Hungary / Turkey / Greece 22. Romania 23. Spain 24. Ukraine 25. Russia

26. India 27. Panama 28. France 29. Peru 30. Kenya / Belgium

Acknowledgments

I am grateful for permission to adapt in this *Pleasury* some items that have appeared in my Pocket Books, Gibbs Smith, and Marion Street Press books. Thousands of thanks to Eileen Breedlove and Charlie Patton for their loving labors to make this book the very best it could be.

Art credits: covers and Teddy Bear by Todd Smith; *Introduction:* The Thinker in the Gates of Hell by Auguste Rodin; *I Never Metaphor I Didn't Like:* raining cats and dogs by Charles Patton; *Noah's Ark:* Italianate mural painting of Noah's Ark; *Land, Sea, Air, and Beyond:* clouds by Novoklimov; moon image from George Méliès, *Le Voyage dans la Lune* (1902); *Our Sporty English Language:* U.S. postage stamps for the 1996 Centennial Olympic Games; *The Annals of Science:* Albert Einstein and Marie Skłodowska Curie; *Classical Words:* first-century BCE bronze statue of Aule Metele, known as The Orator; *Sacred Words:* Adam and Eve, by Albrecht Dürer, 1504; *Location, Location:* Hamburg, by Aliasdoobs, commons license; Frankfurt, by Markus Schüller, commons license.

AUTHOR BIOGRAPHY

Richard Lederer is the author of more than fifty books about language, history, and humor, including his best-selling *Anguished English* series and his current books, *The Gift of Age, A Treasury of Halloween Humor, A Treasury of Christmas Humor,* and *Richard Lederer's Ultimate Book of Literary Trivia.* He is a founding co-host of *A Way With Words,* broadcast on Public Radio.

Dr. Lederer's column, *Lederer on Language,* appears in newspapers and magazines throughout the United States. He has been named International Punster of the Year and Toastmasters International's Golden Gavel winner.

He lives in San Diego with his wife, Simone van Egeren.

richardhlederer@gmail.com / www.verbivore.com

www.ingramcontent.com/pod-product-compliance
Lightning Source LLC
Chambersburg PA
CBHW071653090426
42738CB00009B/1516